Christa Wolf

Der geteilte Himmel

Karin McPherson

Senior Lecturer in German,
University of Edinburgh

University of Glasgow
French and German Publications
1995

University of Glasgow French and German Publications

Series Editors:
Mark G. Ward (German)
Geoff Woollen (French)

Consultant Editors :
Colin Smethurst
Kenneth Varty

Modern Languages Building, University of Glasgow,
Glasgow G12 8QL, Scotland.

First published 1995.

Printed by Castle Cary Press, Yeovil, Somerset, BA20 2HP.

ISBN 0 85261 449 7

Contents

CHAPTER ONE

a) Reading between the lines : a biography Christa Wolf 1929 - 1989

Christa Wolf was thirty-two years old and married with two daughters (born 1952 and 1956), when she published her first slim work of fiction, *Moskauer Novelle*, in 1961. This was followed two years later by her second, much more substantial book *Der geteilte Himmel*. Between 1955 and 1962 she had already held several key posts in the field of cultural policy making, as member of the Executive (Vorstandsmitglied) of the East German Writers' Union (Schriftstellerverband), as head reader (Cheflektorin) of a publishing house which dealt with young authors, Verlag Neues Leben, and editor of the literary magazine *Neue Deutsche Literatur*. She had reviewed and evaluated works of new writers, and made decisions as to whether or not a work was worthy of being published in the cultural and political climate of the socialist society with which she closely identified in those days.

Following the guidelines for writers and artists, issued by the Party through their First Secretary Walter Ulbricht at the First Bitterfeld Conference[1] of 1959, she had joined the workers at a carriage building factory at Halle (Waggonwerk Ammendorf) and had gained her first experience as a budding writer through close observation and collaboration with the team to which she was attached, her Brigade. She thus obtained first-hand knowledge of the problems faced by a vital industry in the years when the GDR began to recover from the heavy reparations paid after the war to the Soviet Union (a taboo theme for literature of those years). She witnessed problems which had to be overcome in coping with shortage of material and parts, with a diminishing workforce through defections to the West, with problems of personalities, all set against the constant pressure from a centralized

[1] In 1959, a conference took place in a factory at Bitterfeld near Halle, where writers, publishers and workers were assembled by the Party and new guidelines pronounced for the writers, in an attempt to create an indigenous GDR literature, based on closer contacts of the intellectuals with the ruling class of workers and farmers. Writers were urged to gain direct experience in factories, on building sites and collective farms, and workers were encouraged to try their hand at writing. The author Werner Bräunig, (later disgraced at the 11th Plenum), issued the slogan "Greif zur Feder, Kumpel, die sozialistische Nationalkultur braucht dich!". See D. Tate, *The East German Novel*, (Bath, 1984): Chap. 3, 'Continuity and Conflict in the GDR's Development', pp. 90 ff.

government and Party to increase production output. Pressures of this kind had led to the workers' uprising on 17 June 1953, and still had not been resolved in the late 1950s. The sealing of the border to the West, with the building of the Wall on 13 August 1961, forced workers and Party to regard the problems as inherent to the GDR. Whereas before the 13 August 1961, GDR citizens exercised a choice either to stay in the GDR and put up with economic and social restraints, or escape (through the open border in Berlin) to the thriving economy of post-war West Germany, they were now faced with the task of making the best of living conditions under Socialism. The Party was increasingly aware of the need to improve standards of living to compete with the success of Capitalism. The working population, no longer content with idealistic goals, wanted to see material benefits for their efforts. The unrest and discontent among factory workers belonged to Christa Wolf's experiences at the factory at Halle. Her allegiance to the Party which she had joined as a student in 1949, the year in which the GDR was founded, was put to a stringent test by these experiences. The strength of her belief in the Party and in the future socialist society is reflected in the fact that she was put forward as candidate for the Central Committee of the SED in 1963, joining the leading ranks of the Party as a non-voting member. Equally significant is the fact that her candidature was not renewed in 1967. It is during those intervening years between her two major works of the 1960s, *Der geteilte Himmel* and *Nachdenken über Christa T.* (1968) that she began to question her political outlook. This had serious implication for her writing which underwent profound changes in those years.

To understand both the eagerness with which Christa Wolf embraced Socialism in her early twenties, and her profound moral scruples with regard to her own position in a society from which she felt increasingly alienated in her thirties, we have to take into consideration her childhood and youth under National Socialism.

It was not until the mid-1970s, when she was in her forties, that Christa Wolf revealed aspects of her own childhood and youth through the fictional character of Nelly Jordan in the substantial prose narrative, *Kindheitsmuster* (1976). Christa Wolf, born Christa Ihlenfeld on 18 March 1929, was of a similar age to her central character, and like her she grew up in the middle-sized town of Landsberg an der Warthe, just east of the river Oder, which became the Polish town Gorzow Wielkopolski after the end of World War II. Like Nelly, Christa Ihlenfeld was the daughter of lower middle class, hardworking parents who ran a local grocery shop which, though threatened by the economic slump of the late twenties and early thirties, recovered and did well after Hitler came to power in 1933. Not surprisingly, Christa's parents, like Nelly's, joined the party out of a sense of duty and a wish not to remain outsiders in a nation swept off its feet by promises of economic and social welfare. Early signs of anti-semitism and preparation for war were suppressed by the desire, in both the parents and the daughter, to do well and be accepted. Young Christa, like most children of her age, joined the Hitler Youth movement and, if, as we may assume, Nelly is modelled on her, eagerly involved herself in the spirit of competition, taking on the post of a group leader. Growing up in a small town and a closeknit family, somewhat remote from the centres of National Socialism, Berlin and Munich, Christa developed her own form of acquiescing in "ordinary fascism". The beginning of the war in 1939 revealed first ominous cracks in the secure childhood heaven. In the novel, the calling-up of the father, a veteran of World War I, and her mother's loud protest at this event, are registered by the child as signs that all is not well with the system.

In January 1945, Nelly Jordan, like Christa Ihlenfeld, became one of a vast number of refugees who were arbitrarily uprooted and resettled where the end of the war caught up with them. In both fiction and real life, this happened to be Mecklenburg (Gammelin), a province in North Germany which was briefly occupied by British and American troops, before it became the Soviet-occupied Zone and, on 7th October 1949, part of the newly founded German Democratic Republic. Christa Ihlenfeld, like Nelly, worked as clerk for the newly appointed town mayor before resuming her grammar school education which had been disrupted by the end of the war. At that time, she contracted tuberculosis and had to spend several months in hospital. All these experiences coinciding with her adolescence led to a deep emotional crisis. *Kindheitsmuster* does not linger on this period, but the earlier book, *Nachdenken über Christa T.*, offers glimpses into the depth of the crisis and disorientation.

In 1947, Christa Ihlenfeld moved to Bad Frankenhausen (Kyffhäuser) where she finished her school education, taking her Abitur in 1949. During that period, she also worked for a short time as untrained primary school teacher, to fill a gap created by dismissal of schoolteachers who had been members of the National Socialist Party during the Third Reich. In 1949, she took two important steps which were to determine the course her life took over the next decades: she enroled as a student of German and Philosophy, first at the University of Jena (where Schiller had taught and which was named after him), a year later at the Karl-Marx University of Leipzig, and she became a member of the ruling political party of the GDR, the SED.[2] When asked in later years why she joined the Party in the first place, and why she remained a member in spite of her increasingly critical attitude, she defended her decision as one taken in good faith, initiated by her reading of the "classics", Marx, Lenin and Engels during and after 1949, at a time when she was both mentally in need of guidance and emotionally at her most receptive. In several interviews conducted with her during the 1970s and 80s she explained the background.[3] The deep disillusionment and shock created by the collapse of National Socialism had led her, like many who had grown up under strict political guidance and without help from parents in developing a critical attitude towards a corrupt system, to reach for a substitute authority. This she found not only in the teachings of Marx, Lenin and Engels, but even more in the examples of the older generation of Marxist writers who returned to Germany after spending the years when Hitler ruled Germany in exile, because of their stongly held anti-fascist beliefs. Among them, the most important influence for Christa Wolf was Anna Seghers, author of *Das siebte Kreuz* (first published in Germany in 1946, but written in exile), one of the earliest and most perceptive books about the effects of Fascism among the ordinary people in Germany of the 1930s.

Christa Wolf only relinquished her membership when the Party failed to take note of the mass exodus of people from the GDR after the opening of the border to the West in Hungary, in the summer of 1989. Her continued Party membership up until that time severely dented her reputation after the collapse of the GDR in 1990, causing a first wave of criticism of her failure to take a decisive anti-government stance in the West German media in 1990.[4]

As a young, impressionable student at Leipzig, Christa Wolf was taught Philosophy and Literature by Hans Mayer and Ernst Bloch, who represented a form of enlightened humanist Marxism. But their influence was soon eclipsed by the more orthodox Socialist Realism of the Hungarian Marxist philosopher Georg Lukács. However, Christa

[2] The Socialist Unity Party (SED) had been formed in the Soviet-occupied Zone in 1946, through merging the German Communist and Socialist Parties (KPD and and SPD). This was effectively a severance from the two separate parties which continued to exist in the Western Zones. It caused strong frictions, particularly in Berlin with its post-war division into four Occupation Zones, leading to an escalation of the alienation between East and West.

[3] See, among others, T. Hörnigk, 'Gespräch mit Christa Wolf' in T.H., *Christa Wolf*, (Göttingen, 1989), pp. 7 ff.

[4] The controversy focussed on a debate surrounding C. Wolf's text *Was bleibt* (1990), documented, with comments, in *Der deutsch-deutsche Literaturstreit oder 'Freunde, es spricht sich schlecht mit gebundener Zunge'. Analysen und Materialien* , ed. K. Deiritz und H. Krauss, (Darmstadt, 1991).

Wolf's great thirst for books was not easily quenched by the official canon of reading, which included the Weimar classics, Goethe and Schiller, but excluded the writers of the early 19th century, Büchner, Kleist and the Romantics. There was a strict ban on modernist authors who had such a profound influence on post-war European literature in the West. In her early years, Christa Wolf therefore had no exposure to the works of James Joyce, Virginia Woolf and the American modernists, and Kafka could only be read in secret before the first Kafka Conference in Liblice in 1963. She turned to the Russian and German late 19th century writers, reading Dostoyevsky, Storm and Keller, and to Soviet authors whose country had become a close cultural ally for the GDR.

For Christa Ihlenfeld, the early 1950s were not only intellectually, but also emotionally formative years. Indeed, those two aspects have always been inseparable for her. While a student at Jena, she met and married a fellow student, Gerhard Wolf, who shared her keen interest in literature. This marriage proved to be a strong bond which sustained both partners throughout periods of political and cultural pressures and bore fruit in the literary and critical output of both. In 1952, after the couple had moved to Leipzig where Gerhard Wolf worked as radio critic, their first daughter Annette was born while Christa Wolf was still a student. She graduated in 1953 and, turning down the chance to pursue an academic career, first moved to Berlin to work for the Writers' Union, thereby beginning her career in cultural politics. As editor and publishers' reader, Christa Wolf kept close to the official literary criteria of Socialist Realism and applied them, although never indiscriminately, in her reviews and testimonials of contemporary works.

Her enthusiastic belief in the future of the new socialist society persuaded her, like many writers and artists of her generation, of the need for a prescriptive, partisan literature. But her own literary preference, strengthened by the critical ideas absorbed through the teachings of Mayer and Bloch, had already given her a sense of literary excellence as found, for instance, in the narrative style of Thomas Mann. This conflicted with her own professed political outlook even before she herself began to write fiction.

With two young children, Christa Wolf was an example for those women who aimed at combining a family with a career, particularly important in a society which had equality and equal opportunities written into its Constitution. The practical problems and dilemmas which equality brought for women in trying to reconcile these roles are revealed in her many references to the family, especially her children and, since the late 1970s, her grandchildren. Children appear in all her fictional and many of her non-fictional works, with the notable exceptions of her earliest books, *Moskauer Novelle* and *Der geteilte Himmel*.

In 1959, the family moved to Halle where both Christa and Gerhard Wolf worked for the publishing house Mitteldeutscher Verlag. Together they edited two anthologies of prose and poetry written during the first ten years of the GDR, entitled *Wir, unsere Zeit*. This was thc first of a number of joint ventures by the couple after their script for the film *Die Toten bleiben jung* in 1958, based on Anna Seghers' first post-war novel published in the GDR. In collaboration with their namesake Konrad Wolf, one of the leading film directors in the GDR, they wrote the script for the film *Der geteilte Himmel* (1963/64), which was first shown in 1965, and is still considered one of the classic films of the East German DEFA (Deutsche Film-AG) production company.[5] The Wolfs were less lucky with their next joint venture for the State-owned GDR film industry; their script for *Fräulein Schmetterling*, another contemporary subject, ran into difficulties with the authorities at the time of the 11th Plenum and remained unfinished, with no records in the archives. It was not until 1972 that the Wolfs went into publication together again, with the book and filmscript on the subject of Till Eulenspiegel, a German Robin Hood.

While Gerhard Wolf made a name for himself as an editor of lyric poetry and biographer of Hölderlin and Bobrowski, Christa Wolf quickly gained a high profile as an author of contemporary prose. With *Der geteilte Himmel*, her work became the subject of a heated critical debate in East and West Germany, and her international reputation was established by the late 1960s, with her novel *Nachdenken über Christa T.*. With each subsequent novel, essay or interview she aroused public debate and her work was taken as a moral indicator and critical yardstick for those who observed the GDR from outside, as well as for the readership in her own country, notwithstanding the changing fortunes of the treatment her work received by GDR critics and politicians.

Although Gerhard Wolf never tried to match Christa's high profile and public image, he made important contributions through his sensitive discovery and promotion of the finer vibrations which lyric poetry added to the clamour of public debate surrounding prose and drama in the GDR. And although he stayed in the background when Christa Wolf

[5] For a brief history of the GDR film industry and what has become of it since 1989, see R. Kilborn, 'Winds of Change in GDR Film Making', *GDR Monitor*, (23, 1990), 13 ff.

was seen as representing GDR literature and politics during their more and more frequent visits to the West, he bore the brunt of the political wrath incited by the protest letter which the Wolfs and eleven other writers signed after the GDR expelled the political song writer Wolf Biermann in 1976. Gerhard Wolf was stripped of his Party membership and expelled from the Writers' Union, whereas Christa Wolf escaped more lightly, losing her place on the Executive Committee of the Writers' Union in Berlin. The story *Was bleibt* which was published in 1990, although written in the late 1970s as an account of the period in Christa Wolf's life after the Biermann crisis, when she was shadowed by the Stasi and betrayed by some fellow writers, reveals that she remained by no means unscathed. To her readers this was already clear when her novella *Kein Ort. Nirgends* appeared in 1979. There she conveys the plight of the writers ousted by their society through the fictitious encounter of two figures from the early 19th century, Karoline von Günderrode and Heinrich von Kleist, who both ended their lives through suicide. Since the 1960s, the Wolfs had published both fiction and essays which brought hitherto neglected literary figures of the period of Romanticism to the attention of their readers. Some of this was reflected in a volume of essays published in 1985 with the title *Ins Ungebundene gehet eine Sehnsucht. Gesprächsraum Romantik.*

From the early 1980s onwards, Christa Wolf focussed her attention on wider contemporary issues, as she was more and more concerned with the role of women and the nuclear arms race: both made her work once again the centre of political debate in the West, while her own country ignored her, or at best treated her with guarded scepticism. Increasingly, however, her books commanded a wide readership among people on both sides of the political divide.

In the early 1980s, she was the first East German author to be appointed guest professor to the prestigious Chair of Poetics of the Johann-Wolfgang-Goethe Universität at Frankfurt am Main, a post which had also been held by the Austrian Ingeborg Bachmann, whose work Wolf had closely followed since the mid-1960s, and by Heinrich Böll, a life-long admirer of Wolf's moral commitment. Wolf's *Frankfurter Vorlesungen* consisted of four lectures in the form of essays, in which she related her experiences during a journey to Greece in search of the subject of her next book, *Kassandra*. The mythological figure of Cassandra who against her will foresees the destruction through warfare of her own people, the Trojans, stands for the woman caught between the ancient peaceful matriarchial and the modern aggressive patriarchal systems. In her lectures, Wolf used the form of personal letters and diaries for an open discussion of her concern for the future of mankind in the face of the escalation of the nuclear arms race. Her stance on unilateral nuclear disarmament in one of the lectures earned her once again the Party's disfavour. For the publication of the four lectures and the story of Cassandra, the East German authorities insisted on cutting vital passages from the text before it was allowed to appear in 1983, after the - uncensored - West German edition. Significantly, as the Cold War drew to its closing stages in the later 1980s, the 6th edition of *Kassandra. Vier Vorlesungen. Eine Erzählung* (Berlin and Weimar, 1988) had the cuts restored.

Like the last two of the *Kassandra* lectures, Wolf's stories of the later 1980s, *Störfall* and *Sommerstück* are set in her country retreat in Mecklenburg where the Wolfs had acquired a thatched farmhouse in the village of Meteln near Güstrow. The house not only provided a refuge from the hectic political atmosphere of East Berlin, their main residence, it also allowed Christa Wolf to take root once more in a rural environment, not far from the place where she had spent a significant part of her adolescence after the end of the war. Here she was able to write and, as she felt increasingly alienated from the political developments in the GDR, discuss her doubts and concerns with her family and closest friends whom she trusted. How precarious and misguided this trust could be has been revealed since access has been gained to the files held by the East German secret police, the Stasi (Staatssicherheitsdienst). Some of the friends who gathered in the rural peace of the Wolf's home have turned out to have been in the employ of the Stasi as informers. The house itself was completely destroyed by fire in the hot summer of 1983, an event which is ominously anticipated in the novella *Sommerstück*, her last fiction published while the GDR was still in existence. It was written in several stages between the mid 1970s and the early 1980s, revised in 1987, and finally appeared in 1989.

Here, as in other later works, Christa Wolf returns to the form of the fictional diary, with strong autobiographical undercurrents, which she had first adopted in the early 1960s, in *Dienstag, der 27. September* (1960), and in her remarkable short story 'Juninachmittag' of 1965. In 1962, the Wolf family had moved away from the industrial town of Halle (near Leipzig and Bitterfeld on the river Saale) to Berlin, to a house in the garden suburb of Kleinmachnow. This rural setting close to the border forms the subject of the story. The narrator, a mother of two children, with a husband reassuringly in the background who tends the garden and discusses literary topics with her, reflects on her own emotional turbulences, sparked off by private and public events in her environment. Written in the first-person narrative without plot or apparent political message, it was in itself a grave breach of the prevailing literary convention of Socialist Realism. Moreover, the introspective perspective of the narrator and the story's middle-class milieu did not comply with the political consciousness demanded of writers in the GDR of the 1960s.

Christa Wolf had taken the bold step of offending against the cultural prescriptions to which she had adhered only a few years earlier. An established writer after the publication of her first two books, *Moskauer Novelle* and *Der geteilte Himmel*, recipient of several prestigious literary prizes in the GDR, member of the Executive Committee of the Writers' Union, and a candidate for the Central Committee of the SED, Christa Wolf expressed controversial views at the Second Bitterfeld Conference of 1964, and she also spoke critically at the notorious meeting of the 11th Plenum of the SED in 1965 when hitherto successful and promising authors and filmmakers were severely criticised by the Party over their alleged betrayal of socialist cultural policies.[6] The core of Wolf's criticism, also a form of self-correction, concerned the suppression of the author's individuality and personal experience through orthodox ideology. Far from wanting to undermine the Party, Wolf was hoping to convince fellow members of the Writers' Union of the need to make the individual the measure of society, and not vice versa, as was the declared policy of Socialism, reflected in the Party slogan "Vom Ich zum Wir". She warned of the danger of making this rule into a fetish and demanded instead that writers should be allowed to draw on the rich fund of their experience within the framework of the new society in which she believed fervently. This was in breach of the Socialist Realist principles of class-consciousness ("Klassenbewußtsein") and partisanship ("Parteilichkeit"), and of the decree of the Bitterfeld Conference which stated that workers and peasants were the most worthy subject of literature.

Christa Wolf did not remain a candidate for the Central Committee after the next Party Congress of 1967. Her work during the second half of the 1960s was written, as it were, "against the grain" of the GDR. Her stories and essays, among them the first major essay reflecting her own approach to writing prose from an individual, not a partisan point of view, *Lesen und Schreiben* of 1968, were not published until the 1970s. *Nachdenken über Christa T.*, the story again told by a first-

[6] Much of this has come to light since the opening of the Wall and the end of the GDR. It is documented in the volume *Kahlschlag. Das 11. Plenum des ZK der SED 1965*, (Berlin 1991). This includes the transcript of Christa Wolf's impromptu speech ('Diskussionsbeitrag', pp. 334 - 344) and her memories of the events at the Plenum ('Erinnerungsbericht', pp. 263 ff).

person narrator, of a female friend who had died, still in her prime, of leukaemia, but whose main problem had been that she had not been able to adapt to the norms set by the GDR society of the 1950s and 60s, is a kind of subtext to Christa Wolf's own development. But she survived, remaining politically involved through writing the story of Christa T. based on personal experiences and memories, thereby finding her own level of narrative. It is also the story of a whole generation of young Germans who embraced Socialism, and whose Utopian hopes where dashed with the crushing of the Hungarian uprising of 1956, and the revelations of the purges under Stalin at the XXth Party Congress in the Soviet Union of the same year. Political mistakes are not openly discussed in the book, but their psychological effects on the young adults trying to build a new society are revealed in all their devastating effects. This kind of searching writing did not fit into the cultural and political programme of the GDR. More light is shed on Christa Wolf's situation during the late 60s through documents published recently, revealing the struggles surrounding the publication of *Nachdenken über Christa T.*.[7]

The early 1970s brought a change in the cultural climate in the GDR, together with the new Party leadership. In 1971 Erich Honecker took over the posts of First Party Secretary from Walter Ulbricht, a faithful follower of Stalin beyond his death, who had led the country's affairs since 1949 and had exerted a strong influence over the cultural policies of the country. Honecker, in a speech at the Plenary session of the Central Committee of the SED in 1971, pronounced that, on the firm basis of Socialism, there could be no more taboos in literature and art, both in respect of subject matter and of style. This was eagerly interpreted by writers, critics and publishers as a sign of liberalisation, and hitherto unpublished books appeared, among them Ulrich Plenzdorf's *Die neuen Leiden des jungen W.*, and Christa Wolf's *Unter den Linden. Drei unwahrscheinliche Geschichten* (1974), her first venture into the surreal, dream and science fiction. Also in the early 70s, her essays came out, under the title *Lesen und Schreiben*, and *Nachdenken über Christa T.* was republished and went into several editions in quick succession. Wolf also started to give frank interviews in East and West Germany, which have since been published together with her collected essays under the title *Die Dimension des Autors* (1986).

The 1970s were also a time of extensive travel in the West for the

[7] See *Dokumentation zu Christa Wolfs Nachdenken über Christa T.*, ed A. Drescher, (Hamburg 1991). The recently published correspondence between Christa Wolf and Brigitte Reimann contains additional evidence of the struggles in getting the book accepted. *Sei gegrüßt und lebe. Brigitte Reimann/ Christa Wolf. Eine Freundschaft in Briefen 1964-1973*, ed. A. Drescher (Berlin, 1993).

Wolfs. Already in the 1960s, they had visited those countries with which the GDR had cultural and political links, the Soviet Union, Poland, Finland and Yugoslavia, but also France and West Germany, even though diplomatic relations were not formally established between the Federal Republic and the GDR until 1972. In 1974 Christa Wolf first went to the USA, as Writer-in-Residence at Oberlin College/Ohio. She visited Stockholm in 1973 and 1978, as member of the International PEN Congress, and in 1978 Christa and Gerhard Wolf spent two weeks in Scotland as visiting lecturers in the German Department at the University of Edinburgh. A visit to Greece in search of the Ancient World in 1980 was followed by another stay in USA in 1983 where Christa Wolf was visiting professor and received an Honorary Doctorate from the Ohio State University, Columbus, Ohio. In recognition of her work, she was made Honorary Fellow of the Modern Languages Association of America in 1985. In 1987, she was visiting professor for creative writing at the Technical University of Zurich.

Her commitment to the Peace Movement, reflected in the lectures and the story *Kassandra* compelled her to take part in three successive peace meetings held jointly by writers from East and West Germany in the early 1980s, "Berliner Begegnung" in East Berlin in 1981, a meeting in The Hague in 1983 and in Berlin in 1987.

By the 1980s, Christa Wolf had become one of the most publicly acclaimed literary figures in the post-war era. She was a member of International Pen, of the Akademie der Künste der DDR (since 1974) and of the Akademie der Künste Berlin, West, (since 1981), as well as of the European Academy of Arts and Sciences, Paris (1984). She had received many prestigious prizes, among them, the Georg-Büchner Preis der deutschen Akademie für Sprache und Dichtung in Darmstadt in 1980, the Friedrich-Schiller-Gedächtnispreis des Landes Baden-Würtemberg, the Österreichische Staatspreis für Europäische Literatur in 1985, the Geschwister-Scholl-Preis of the city of Munich in 1987. She had been awarded an Honorary Doctorate by the University of Hamburg (1985), and she had even been nominated for the Nobel Peace Prize for Literature in the late 1980s.

Against these honours bestowed on her by West Germany, France, Austria and USA, her own country was slow in offering her recognition (after an initial flurry of prizes in the early 1960s). It was only in 1987 that she received the Nationalpreis I. Klasse für Kunst und Literatur from her own Akademie der Künste der DDR.

The latest chapter in her life, the decline and fall of Socialism, has left its mark. She wholeheartedly welcomed the "peaceful revolution" of

1989 in Leipzig (which she called "city of heroes") and East Berlin as a last chance to renew Socialism and restore democracy in its ideal humanist form, and she herself read a proclamation, "Sprache der Wende", on the 4th of November 1989 at the demonstration on Alexanderplatz. But the subsequent events leading towards a single Germany shattered her confidence in human reason. In stark contrast to the special status given to her by the West during the last decades of the GDR, as the upholder of moral and ethical values in Germany, she has been the target of much criticism since Unification, as an intellectual and writer on whom privileges were bestowed in the GDR, who did not protest loudly enough against the abuse of power, thereby implicitly condoning the State. Yet, it was her moral conscience, muted because of her inward-looking nature, but nevertheless audible to the wider readership, which made her a thorn in the flesh of GDR authorities.[8]

Not surprisingly, Christa Wolf's most recently published book, *Auf dem Weg nach Tabou. Texte 1990-1994* (Köln, 1994) is a documentation of her search into the causes for the fall of the GDR, and her own position vis-à-vis the doomed adventure of creating a socialist society. It consist largely of authentic documents, some of which continue in the manner of part-diary, part-fiction which Wolf had first employed in 1960, in her story *Dienstag, der 27. September* which will be discussed below. *Auf dem Weg nach Tabou* must be read as part of the process of analysing her own past in an ongoing attempt to find the truth: a theme that runs through all of Christa Wolf's work.

b) The Writer's Workshop: *Dienstag, der 27 September*

In Christa Wolf's fiction, only her first two works, *Moskauer Novelle* and *Der geteilte Himmel*, have a plot in the conventional sense, a story

[8] To what extent the authorities in her own country distrusted her was revealed by the records of the surveillance of Christa and Gerhard Wolf by the Stasi. Between 1969 and 1980, 20 volumes with 400 different items of reports were collected, and further files from the period after 1980 were destroyed, before they could be passed on to the Gauck-Behörde. (Gauck, a former pastor in the GDR, was put in charge of the team of administrators who grant access to the files after a lengthy process of application.) Christa Wolf's files contained references to her contacts with the Stasi between 1959 and 1962, when she had been approached and asked to give information on individuals as part of her work as editor for the publishing house Mitteldeutscher Verlag. The fact that she did not refuse, and the existence of at least one document under her code name Margarete, put her into the category of those who are now accused of having collaborated with the Stasi as IM (Informeller Mitarbeiter). This once again highlighted her precarious status as the intellectual who had not opposed the system. To put the whole incident into context, Christa and Gerhard Wolf decided to have their files published in 1993. See *Akteneinsicht Christa Wolf. Zerrspiegel und Dialog. Eine Dokumentation*, ed. H. Vinke, (Hamburg 1993).

line or, in Socialist Realist terminology, a "Fabel". Moreover, both stories are set within a clearly defined time-span which, in the case of *Der geteilte Himmel*, almost exactly coincides with the period in the history of the GDR in which the book was written, i.e. the late 1950s and early 60s. There is, however, a significant time-lapse between the events of the story and the actual writing of the book in its final form. This puts a distance between the actual writing and the political events leading up to and culminating in the closing of the border between East and West Germany in 1961. Reflecting back over past events is also an in-built stylistic and structural feature of the book itself, which covers a timespan of two years. This distancing act of reflection is a feature which will occur in all Wolf's later fiction. Moreover, it distinguishes her early story from those contemporary novels which adhere strictly to the guidelines of Socialist Realism with its emphasis on straightforward chronological narrative.

The story of *Der geteilte Himmel* is banal in itself, without the reference to the special situation in which it was conceived. But within the context of the historical circumstances of the time, and in view of the retrospective reflective element added by the author, it succeeds in making a significant comment on the contemporary situation in which a young woman, entering adulthood, finds herself caught up in the crisis precipitated by the GDR's attempts to maintain an identity of its own vis-à-vis the West, in the midst of the Cold War climate. It is in this respect that Wolf added her own experiences to the story, despite this being perhaps the least autobiographical of her works.

In one of her earliest short prose works cast in quasi-diary form, *Dienstag, der 27. September*, first published in 1974, but written in 1960 during the preliminary stages of her work on *Der geteilte Himmel*, Wolf fictionalizes the circumstances under which she, as a young author and mother of two children, conceived the ideas for her book and the difficulties she faces in putting them on paper. The diary sketch describes a day in the life of a young writer, a mother and housewife with a four-year-old daughter on her hands, trying to snatch a moment here and there to return to her manuscript. There is an older daughter who, when returning from school, also demands the mother's attention and adds to the general distractions surrounding the preparations for the birthday party for the younger child on the following day. The husband is present, but does not take part in the hustle and bustle of household and family duties. His role is to be an authority on literary questions, and a dialogue between him and the narrator revolves around questions of art and politics: "unser altes

Thema: Kunst und Revolution, Politik und Kunst, Ideologie und Literatur".[9]

It adds an interesting comment on the dual, even triple role of women in the GDR which had made it one of its basic principles that men and women have equality in their right to work,[10] that in the day-to-day reality, looking after the children and all other household duties are still the responsibility of the mother/narrator. Somehow, in the middle of this chaotic day, this narrator finds time to visit her Brigade, the work-force at the factory where she is given responsibility for cultural matters, to attend one of their political meetings ("Parteigruppensitzung"). In this feature of the story, Wolf, in adhering to the Bitterfelder Weg, draws on her own experience at the Waggonwerk Ammenberg. It is only at the end of the day, when all has quietened down, that the narrator gets a chance to contemplate her own work, a story she is about to write and which has presented her with some difficulties, causing a kind of writer's block. The description of this story, still in its early stages, fits that of the novel *Der geteilte Himmel.*

True to the form of a diary, *Dienstag, der 27. September* is written in the first person, and for those familiar with Wolf's biography, the parallels are unmistakable. There is also a strong link with the style of her story 'Juninachmittag', which was written immediately after *Der geteilte Himmel* and published in 1967. Between these two prose works, Wolf had written a text for broadcasting, commissioned by West German radio in 1964, entitled 'Tagebuch-Arbeitsmittel und Gedächtnis'.[11] If we regard *Dienstag, der 27. September* as autobiography, it is clear that the author experienced considerable difficulties in merging two themes under one single universal idea. The two themes are the love between a young country girl and a newly qualified scientist, but "er bekommt sie am Ende nicht", and the story of a socialist work brigade at a railway carriage factory. The two strands

[9] C. Wolf, *Gesammelte Erzählungen*, (Darmstadt and Neuwied, 1974), p. .27.

[10] See *Frauen in der DDR. Auf dem Wege zur Gleichberechtigung?*, Friedrich-Ebert-Stiftung, (Bonn, 1987). "Bereits in der ersten Verfassung der DDR von 1949 war die Gleichberechtigung von Frau und Mann festgeschrieben worden ... Die Verfassung von 1968, fortgeschrieben 1974, übernahm die Aussagen zur Gleichberechtigung von 1949 vom Inhalt her." (p. 6) "In der kommunistischen Ideologie gilt als Voraussetzung für das Erreichen der Gleichberechtigung der Frau ihre Berufstätigkeit. Nur dadurch gewinne sie ihre allgemeine Unabhängigkeit, ihr Leben frei zu gestalten. Deshalb, so betont die SED immer wieder, habe man bei der Verwirklichung der Gleichberechtigung in der Sowjetischen Besatzungszone Deutschlands ... und späteren DDR damit begonnen, der Frau den Weg in die Berufstätigkeit auf allen Gebieten zu ebnen." (p. 7)

[11] Published in 1972 in the first East German edition of *Lesen und Schreiben* (Berlin and Weimar, 1968), reprinted in *Die Dimension des Autors*, (Berlin and Weimar, 1986), Vol. 1, 13ff..

of the story are loosely connected through a third character, a young master craftsman ("ein junger Meister"), who is demoted by the Party to work with the brigade, in order to rectify his past mistakes, and who competes with the young doctor for the love of the girl. (*Erzählungen*, 39-40)

The narrator of *Dienstag* sees herself confronted by two problems: firstly, how to raise the story of the brigade from the level of reportage (a popular genre at the time of writing) to that of narrative fiction, and secondly, how to give the banal love story an ideological dimension, a superstructure or, in accordance with Marxist literary theory, a universal application or "Überidee". In the context of the early 1960s, we recognize the difficulties created by the demands made on writers after the First Bitterfeld Conference (1959), to portray the problems of workers and use the workplace as settings for their fiction, when the authors themselves had very little first-hand experience of either. This became all the more difficult when these same writers discovered insoluble problems in the state-run economy. This created a grave conflict as to whether to write the truth or give a positive picture of the situation. The prescriptive directives of the Party regarding Socialist Realism implied that stories had to be written from a partisan point of view and in a manner easily accessible to the ordinary reader, setting positive examples through the characters and their development in order to help the cause of Socialism. It is not surprising, therefore, that the narrator in *Dienstag* feels that she has reached an impasse, and her deliberations allow the reader to reflect on the conflict that arises where the clear remit of the Party on both subject and method of writing clashed with the writer's own experience and perception.

The importance of personal experience ("Erfahrung") is discussed in detail between husband and wife in the prose sketch, in particular the question of the extent to which one can control experience, regardless of social background and individual character. (*Erzählungen*, 27) The significance which Christa Wolf herself attaches to personal experience is emphasised, not only through the diary form, but also in the detailed descriptions of the writer's own family through ordinary everyday events. That conflicts can arise out of the most ordinary situations is illustrated when the mother is forced to deal with her four-year-old's natural curiosity and questions. When they overhear a conversation in the doctor's waiting room between three elderly women about advantages and disadvantages of living in East as opposed to West Germany, the narrator avoids explicit comment rather than lie to the child. She is more open with herself when revealing some of the problems raised by the Brigade, both at a personal level and with regard to serious shortcomings in the production process which threaten to bring work to a standstill. These, apparently insoluble, problems observed by the narrator are in direct conflict with the official version put out by the Party, of an ever-increasing record production in the GDR. Undue demands for production increases under impossible conditions had led to East German workers' uprising in 1953, interpreted and supported by the West as a demand for freedom and unification. It was quickly crushed by the East German government with the help of Soviet tanks.[12] The final bill for these problems, which were never allowed to be openly discussed and which continued to bedevil GDR industry came with the collapse of most heavy industry in the final phase of the country in the late 1980s.

A comparison between *Dienstag* and *Der geteilte Himmel*, with regard to problems encountered by the Brigade Ermisch and the relegated former leader Meternagel, reveals that Christa Wolf herself did not entirely eliminate all references to these problems in her finished version, although they are toned down and seen as a necessary stage in the development towards a better future. Two further themes of the finished story are missing from the diary sketch. One is the reference to the first man put into space by the Russians, Yuri Gagarin, an event which gains considerable significance in giving the book its air of optimism regarding future developments in science and technology, as the basis for the economic and social system of the whole Eastern Bloc. The other is the theme of "Republikflucht", a topical, though controversial subject in the 1960s before the closing of the border. Problems were often evaded by people, unwilling to accept the socialist system, leaving the country through the open border in Berlin, thereby putting a heavy burden on those who stayed.

In developing the individual characters, Manfred Herrfurth, the "young scientist" of the diary sketch, is given considerable weight in the

[12] 17 June 1953 has gone down as an historical date only in West Germany where it was a national holiday until 1989. It had a street named after it, running through the centre of West Berlin to the Brandernburger Tor, the dividing line between East and West. The facts are that, what started as a protest of East German workers against unreasonable increases in production norms by the government under Ulbricht, was extended to a cry for free elections and the resignation of the Ulbricht government. Workers from 250 industrial plants in the GDR took part, and when Ulbricht called in Soviet tanks, it came to bloody confrontations and deaths. The repercussions for those involved were severe, and Ulbricht's government remained solid. References to the events in East German literature were suppressed by the censors. Brecht's *Buckower Elegien* were written under the shadow of the events which brought disillusionment to those who believed in the humane nature of Socialism. Stefan Heym's novel *5 Tage im Juni* with its detailed and fair treatment was published only in the West (Munich, 1974). In the 1980s, authors began to make oblique reference to the events, among them Christoph Hein in his novel *Der fremde Freund* (1983); West German edition: *Drachenblut*.

finished novel through being the focus of the ideological struggle in deciding whether to stay in the GDR or move to the West. It is this theme which turns the banal love story into a conflict of tragic dimensions.

Manfred is given the role of the sceptic in the book, the devil's advocate who casts doubt on the Utopian concept of the unstoppable progress of Socialism towards a better future. His counterpart and rival in the novel is Wendland, the "young master craftsman" of *Dienstag, der 27. September*, a convinced and upright exponent of the belief in the inherent strength of Socialism. The "young girl from the country", in the novel the central character Rita, is caught between these conflicting attitudes. As the young, naive, impressionable girl, she is convinced that the future of humanity lies with Socialism, recognizing the inherent flaws and conflicts only when it is too late to avert the catastrophe of losing Manfred to life in the West. But Wolf does not allow her main character to be destroyed. The close links Rita has formed with her Brigade, the factory workers and their day-to-day struggles, play a decisive part in her recovery. She matures and her faith in human nature gains the upper hand, giving the book its optimistic perspective. This treatment of a delicate theme was very much in character with Wolf's own ideological outlook at the time of writing the book.

b) The Literary Context of *Der geteilte Himmel*

In a number of books written around the time of *Der geteilte Himmel*, the choice between two conflicting ideologies is usually presented in black-and-white terms by authors committed to the "Aufbau" phase of Socialism. A prime example is Anna Seghers' novel *Die Entscheidung* (1959), which Christa Wolf had certainly read. In the early 1960s, after the building of the Wall, the topic began to be treated in a different way with a less clear-cut scenario by a number of authors. Erwin Strittmatter's *Ole Bienkopp* and Brigitte Reimann's *Die Geschwister* appeared in the same year as *Der geteilte Himme*l. Both deal with the conflicts caused by the choice between East and West, and the personal sacrifices involved, leaving a grey area around the actual decision. Brigitte Reimann, born in 1933, had established her reputation as an important first-generation GDR writer with her earlier novel *Ankunft im Alltag* (1961) which gave its name "Ankunftsliteratur" to a whole era in GDR literature. This term describes those works which dealt with everyday reality, after the difficult phase of building a new society of the 1950s.[13] In *Die Geschwister* (1963), Reimann, like Wolf, chooses a female protagonist, but the decision for or against a life in the GDR is left to the male character, in this case an older brother, a scientist like Manfred. In describing the poignant effects the decision to leave would have on the sister, Reimann draws on her own experience, but she alters the actual events in letting the brother change his mind and be persuaded by a male friend and staunch Party member to stay in the GDR. For Reimann's female protagonist, as for Rita, the GDR represents the best of all possible worlds. The similarities between the books by Wolf and Reimann lie mainly in the focus on the female perspective, as well as in the persuasive power of Socialism, in each case represented by a young working-class male character with an engaging, if awkward personality, clearly carrying the authors' sympathies. Both authors, young women who were very close in their outlook to each other and to their female characters, were aware that their belief in the GDR was a matter of faith, and that intellectual and rational arguments had no power over those who did not share it.

Another contemporary of Wolf and Reimann, Uwe Johnson, depicted the theme of "Republikflucht" in his early novel *Mutmaßungen über Jakob* in the manner of a detective story, beginning with the death of the central character after his return from a - failed or aborted - attempt to find his girlfriend who had left for the West. Johnson uses a multiple perspective, introducing a number of characters, both East and West German, in search for the reasons behind Jakob's death. Johnson broke with several taboos in the GDR literature of the time. Above all, his book was devoid of a partisan perspective, and his characters were not portrayed as examplary figures in the way it was expected of authors by the Party. Not surprisingly, therefore, the book was refused publication in the GDR, and Johnson left the country where he had strong roots and went to live in West Germany, USA and finally England.[14] In both theme and treatment, Johnson's *Mutmaßungen über*

[13] B. Reimann, *Ankunft im Alltag*, (Berlin, 1961). B. Reimannn, *Die Geschwister*, (Berlin, 1963).

[14] The authors of *Deutsche Literaturgeschichte. Von den Anfängen bis zur Gegenwart*, (Stuttgart, 4/1992), pp. 476-77, regard Johnson's early works, written before 1959, as the true beginnings of a modern literature in the GDR: "Es markiert, auch wenn für die Leser seines Landes damals nicht nachvollziehbar, einsam und unüberhörbar den Beginn der Moderne in der Erzählliteratur der DDR. Dieses Erstbgeburtsrecht muß Johnson nachdrücklich zugesprochen werden, ohne damit die Verdienste von Christa Wolf, Fritz Rudolf Fries oder Ulrich Plenzdorf schmälern zu wollen." *Ingrid Babendererde*, Johnson's earliest novel, based on his political experience at school and university in the GDR in the 1950s and in which the two main characters leave the GDR in the end, was also refused publication in the GDR and only published in the West after his death. F.R. Fries' picaresque novel *Der Weg nach Oobliadooh*, thematically closely linked to Wolf's book, published and enthusiatically reviewed in West Germany in 1966, did not appear in the GDR until 1989.

Jakob is closer to Wolf's second, equally controversial novel of 1968, *Nachdenken über Christa T.*. It is unlikely that Wolf had read the West German edition of Johnson's novel, which appeared in 1959, before she completed *Der geteilte Himmel*, despite the coincidence that her protagonist, like Johnson's Jakob, is walking along railway lines while meeting with an accident. Wolf, like Johnson, surrounds the accident with an air of mystery, leaving the reader in the dark as to the central character's intentions. Where Wolf differs from Johnson, however, is in her treatment of her character after the accident. Rita survives and is given the opportunity during her convalescence from what appears to have been a severe mental breakdown to understand and come to terms with her immediate past. She leaves the reader in no doubt that, at the end of this process, she has overcome the crisis not through suppression of past events, but through trying to understand and bring to the surface what led to it, even if it means facing up to painful truth. This leaves the character in a sober state of mind, with less youthful spontaneity and blind faith, convincing herself that she has made the right decision in not following Manfred, but instead committing herself to the everyday reality of Socialism. The question which remains open, as in all those works which depict young characters in a situation of conflict, is whether the reader is convinced by their decisions.

CHAPTER TWO

BEYOND SOCIALIST REALISM

a) Aspects of the Narrative

The critical debate surrounding *Der geteilte Himmel* was to a considerable extent generated by the unorthodox narrative structure and perspective which Christa Wolf had employed in her book. Cultural authorities in the 1950s and 1960s had issued a number of strict guidelines for the new novel to which authors were expected to adhere. These rules were set against any attempt to introduce avant-garde styles and structures into writing. The latter were judged as decadent, modernist, even Naturalist and were subsumed under the label "Formalismus" which was regarded as the domain of Western ideology. Consequently, modern authors like Kafka, James Joyce or Virginia Woolf were taboo and banned from the bookshelves. Christa Wolf, as editor and reviewer of contemporary novels, was not only aware of these official guidelines and restrictions for her own writing, but also concerned to encourage others to adhere to them, as part of creating a Socialist consciousness in the readers. The prevailing criteria of Socialist Realism, based on the Soviet model established in the 1930s by Stalin, Zhdanov and other orthodox Party members, were introduced as the official cultural policy of the SED in the early 1950s through the Party leader Walter Ulbricht. Until 1956, the theories of the Hungarian Marxist philosopher and critic Georg Lukács were influential in the development of a theory of writing in the GDR.[1] The normative rules, transmitted to the authors through successive Party Congresses and the Writers' Union, demanded of a novel that it had a plot ("Fabel"), typical rather than individual characters and a strictly linear progressive chronological third-person narrative. In the novels of the 1950s and early 1960s, set in the GDR, the main characters were frequently young adults who grew into the new system of the post-war years under the guidance of older Party members, the "heroes" of the story. The "school of life" was practical work in the factory or in agriculture, the

[1] See W. Emmerich, *Kleine Literaturgeschichte der DDR, 1945-1988*, (Darmstadt, 9/1988), pp. 98-101, 'Sozialistischer Realismus versus Formalismus'. For a more detailed study, see M. Scriven and D. Tate (eds.), *European Socialist Realism*, (Oxford/New York/Hamburg, 1988). See also W. Fähnders, 'Sozialistischer Realismus' in *Brockhaus Enzyklopädie in 24 Bänden*, Vol. 20, (Mannheim, 19/1993), 539 - 41.

aim an education to a new Socialist consciousness, thereby overcoming attitudes which lingered on from what was regarded as the bourgeois or fascist past.[2]

An important theme of the novels of this period is the reference to historical and social changes. This was derived from Lukács' adaptation of theories of Socialist Realism. Lukács based his aesthetic theories on major works by 19th century Russian and French novelists, Tolstoi and Balzac, whose novels were seen as representing a totality of life in a rounded organic structure. Experimentation with more open forms of writing common among modern Western novelists were branded as "Formalism".[3] Social issues are reflected through representative "typical" characters. The author's point of view is present as a definite bias, a partisan line, made unobtrusively clear through the third-person narrative stance. Anna Seghers and Brecht had argued with Lukács in letters written in exile against a rigid adherence to the nineteenth-century model against which they set their own brand of Realism. But Seghers did not wish to create dissent in the anti-fascist camp, and she herself adopted a more orthodox style in her novels written after she returned from exile to live in the GDR. In *Die Toten bleiben jung* (1949) and *Die Entscheidung* (1959) she introduces a wide spectrum of characters and covers an extended period in history in an elaborate and multi-facetted plot. Writing in the third person, she retains the authorial perspective and follows a strict chronology in her narrative. Class conflicts are clearly marked through good and bad characters, her style is conventional, with no recourse to inner monologue, introspection and psychological conflict. Her stories are told plainly and realistically, like fairy tales with didactic morals.

Christa Wolf, despite her admiration for Seghers, did not find her a simple model to follow. In her extensive evaluation of Seghers' work and life in a number of essays, among them 'Glauben and Irdisches' (borrowing the title of an essay by Seghers), written in 1968, the same year as *Lesen und Schreiben*, Wolf shows clear signs of emancipation in

---

[2] Brigitte Reimann's novel *Ankunft im Alltag* (1961) created a model for "Ankunftsliteratur". A group of young school-leavers learned to adapt to the ordinary reality of the workers through a practical year spent at a factory before going to University. Reimann's novel follows in the footsteps of the earlier category of Betriebsroman, a mixture of fiction and reportage reflecting the day-to-day reality of the new social structure of nationalized industry ("Volkseigene Betriebe"), reiterated in the Bitterfelder Weg. Other examples of Bitterfeld literature are: Franz Fühmann, *Kabelkran und Blauer Peter*; Karl-Heinz Jakobs, *Beschreibung eines Sommers*, Erik Neutsch, *Bitterfelder Geschichten* [all 1961]). Edward Claudius' *Menschen an unserer Seite* (1951) was an early example of a novel in an industrial setting in the GDR.

[3] Emmerich, *op. cit.*, p.101.

distinguishing her aims from those of Seghers.[4] Even in her first attempt at writing fiction, *Moskauer Novelle*, she had difficulties in adhering to a partisan authorial point of view and a linear plot. Here already she employed the device of reflecting back over the past from a perspective set in the present, with a female narrator as protagonist. This pattern was then taken up again in a modified and much more subtle form in *Der geteilte Himmel*. The difference from Seghers' work lies in the very structure first employed by Wolf in *Der geteilte Himmel*, with the narrative switching between several time levels, going back and forth between past and present, from first to third person narrative, and using such unorthodox stylistic devices as flashback and collage. The most significant departure lies in the narrative stance adopted by Christa Wolf who lets her protagonist speak, thereby abandoning an objective for a more subjective point of view. Yet, a didactic tendency is recognizable in the way in which Rita arrives at a position where she finds self-realization in adapting to contemporary GDR society and its normal day-to-day reality. The "outer frame" of the story is set off against the main text like a prologue and epilogue, in representing a point of view of the near omniscent narrator, as will be discussed below. These parts not only put the story into its historical and social setting, but also integrate the personalized narrative voice into a wider, more general point of view, a "we". For this Wolf may have taken as her example Seghers' earlier novel *Das siebte Kreuz*.

Despite its concern with social issues, *Der geteilte Himmel* is basically a story about individuals. This is emphasised by the way in which the reader is introduced to the story, in reverse order, following Rita's own gradual process of gaining insight into, and understanding of, the past. Rita's story begins with the final stage after her separation from Manfred, but without anticipating the reassuring ending. Several critics have pointed to the fact that the story takes the form of a catharsis, whereby the protagonist goes through a deep crisis to arrive at an understanding of its causes and achieve a final reintegration into the society as a form of finding herself.[5] The crisis at the beginning

[4] C. Wolf, 'Glauben and Irdisches' in *Die Dimension des Autors*, Vol. 1, 339 ff. This is one of ten essays and reviews Wolf has written on Seghers, all listed together under the heading *Zeitgenossen II*, (*Die Dimension des Autors*, Vol. I), 255 ff.

[5] See S. Hilzinger, *Christa Wolf*, (Stuttgart, 1986), p. 18: "Die Anlage dieser Geschichte verweist auf ein kathartisches Prinzip (Krise-Bewältigung-Integration), wie es in modifizierter Form fast alle Prosawerke Wolfs durchzieht, am deutlichsten in der Geschichte 'Unter den Linden' (1969). Ebenso wie dort ist Ritas Geschichte als Geschichte der Überwindung einer persönlichen Krise mit dem Ziel der gesellschaftlichen Integration angelegt, und ebenso wie dort vollzieht sich dieser Prozeß im Erzählen selber."

(Chapter One opens with Rita wakening in hospital after a period of unconsciousness following her accident), sets in motion a process of self-search through reflection and memory, confronting conflict as a way of coming to terms with the past and finding a way back into society and normal day-to-day living.

Although this may not have been intended by the author, the book is seen on close inspection to offend against almost all rules of Socialist Realism with its retrospective approach and its open outcome for the protagonist, with its narrative perspective from two vantage points, present and past, and with a narrator who looks backward and forward simultaneously, often in mid-chapter. Rita's narrative perspective is further at odds with the Socialist Realist model in that it switches constantly between third and first person. She renounces the position of the omniscient author with an objective, if not also a partisan didactic perspective, and she resorts instead to an unwritten dialogue between author and character. (In her next novel, *Nachdenken über Christa T.* Wolf makes this dialogue into a central theme.) The stylistic implications of this flowing perspective are a change from third to first person pronoun, from "sie" to "ich", often in mid-sentence. It is clear that Wolf was aware of, and wanted to emulate, the modernist stylistic devices of interior monologue or stream of consciousness, or at least a more sophisticated form of introspective writing than her contemporaries in the East, with the notable exception of Uwe Johnson.

The conventional structure of a frame and an inner story ("Rahmenerzählung") is adapted by Wolf to a constant interaction and cross-referencing between the two narrative levels. The narrative follows an associative pattern where present and past events can have the effect of triggering each other off, completely abandoning a linear, forward moving chronology. The narrative level of the past events focusses on the period between Christmas 1959 and August 1961. But there are also frequent flashbacks further into the past, often linked to the point of view of the older characters, Manfred, Wendland, Schwarzenbach and Meternagel. By contrast, Rita's perspective is linked to the level of the present, the period of her recovery in the sanatorium the late summer and autumn of 1961. The prologue and epilogue link past and present, focussing on the year 1961 with the crisis in the Cold War situation between East and West, culminating in the building of the Wall, as a dividing line between before and after. However, this fact is referred to only obliquely as subtext to the actual events. As it is told, Rita's and Manfred's story cannot be divided into before and after the building of the Wall. The rising curve of their relationship coincides with their first summer, its conflict and crisis with the second one. Their final meeting in Berlin, which only confirms the inevitable separation, takes place in August 1961, a week before the closing of the border.

A further striking difference between Wolf's book and earlier Socialist Realist novels lies in the way in which she portrays characters who no longer fit into a simple pattern of black-and-white categories. Through her characterization of Rita and Manfred she adds a dimension of depth and unpredictability to the story. Wolf's move towards a psychological approach in her writing is closely tied to her experimentation with style and must have been due to the influence of the great narrators who were not part of the official canon of GDR literature, Dostoyevsky rather than Gorki, Thomas Mann and Gottfried Keller rather than Goethe and Schiller.

But despite her tentative steps in breaking free from prescriptive narrative patterns, Christa Wolf's book falls far short of the bold steps towards modernist writing taken in Uwe Johnson's *Mutmaßungen über Jakob*. It is therefore not altogether surprising that *Der geteilte Himmel* survived the battle of the critics and censors, and the author was awarded the Heinrich-Mann-Preis in 1963, immediately after it was published. This demonstrates that Wolf's style and treatment were still deemed close enough to the acceptable norm at this stage. Her break with convention and deliberate change to modern writing came with the shorter prose works, 'Juninachmittag' and 'Unter den Linden', which soon followed, as well as with her novel *Nachdenken über Christa T.*.

b) *Der geteilte Himmel* - Prologue and Epilogue

Christa Wolf does not leave her readers in any doubt as regards the time when her story is set: the date, the last days of August 1961, is mentioned in the first line of Chapter 1, (9)[6] immediately bringing to mind another date, 13 August 1961, the building of the Wall and the closure of the border between East and West Germany. But beginning at the first page - three short paragraphs preceding the story itself - the uninitiated reader of today may be at a loss where and when to locate the story. (7) In the first paragraph, an anonymous narrator describes a town, its industrial pollution and its people in a mixture of realism and

[6] This, and all following quotations from *Der geteilte Himmel* refer to the dtv edition of 1982 (15th edition), (Deutscher Taschenbuch Verlag, Munich, 1st edition 1973). The page number is given in brackets. The original GDR edition appeared 1963 in Mitteldeutscher Verlag, Halle/Saale.

metaphor. The town, in the heat of an Indian summer, is personified: "Die Stadt ... atmete heftiger als sonst. Ihr Atem fuhr als geballter Rauch aus hundert Fabrikschornsteinen in den reinen Himmel, aber dann verließ ihn die Kraft, weiterzuziehen."

Those who live in the town are brought closer to the reader through "insider" knowledge of the narrator who identifies with the people in sharing their unrest and frustration. Only the last sentence seems to be that of an omniscent narrator with a more distanced perspective: "Aber die Erde trug sie noch und würde sie tragen, solange es sie gab."

The "we" and "they" in the second and third paragraph are a form of self-address. It includes the narrator as one of the people in the town who, having survived a crisis, are returning to the day-to-day reality of ordinary living. The deadly threat has passed: the unemotional voice in the radio and the inaudible voices whispering danger - people's unspoken fears and premontions - are no longer heard.

In a story which Wolf wrote twenty five years later, *Störfall*, the radio once again has a crucial role as the conveyer of good and bad news, as the narrator listens to the "Nachrichten eines Tages", after the reactor explosion at Chernobyl. One striking difference is that the narrator of *Störfall* is on her own, isolated in her own home, while in the earlier work the experience is shared by all those who live in the town. There are further parallels between the two stories, in particular the way in which ordinary activities are seen to sustain the continuation of life in the face of forces which threaten to extinguish this very life: the threat of impending nuclear war. There is also an expression of faith in the strength-giving forces of the earth, although these no longer hold as much promise in *Störfall*, which was written during the escalation of the Cold War in the 1980s. To the readers of 1963 the reference in *Der geteilte Himmel* to the Cold War tensions, culminating in the building of the Wall, was obvious. What readers perhaps were not prepared for, after the general introduction, was to be thrown in at the deep end in being confronted with Rita's crisis before they knew the outcome. Indeed, readers have to wait until the end of the book to learn from the short epilogue that Rita has fully recovered, ready to take her share of the life-giving strength of ordinary day-to-day living. In these final paragraphs, Wolf not only brings the story down to a personal, yet objective, level by writing from Rita's perspective in the third person, she also narrows down the story by emphasising the importance of the nuclear family: husband, wife and children provide the "friendliness" that Rita is looking for as a source of strength. Yet, the story itself leaves Rita without the immediate prospect of marriage and children.

Her faith that she will have her share in this source of friendliness has almost a hint of resignation: it is the price to be paid for peaceful living: "Aber sie hat keine Angst. Das wiegt alles auf: Daß wir uns gewöhnen, ruhig zu schlafen. Daß wir aus dem vollen leben, als gäbe es übergenug von diesem seltsamen Stoff Leben." (199) The last two sentences are once again spoken by an omniscent narrator who refers back to the "we" of the prologue. It suggests that the reward is there for all to share, - all, that is, who have overcome the crisis and reconciled themselves to what life has to offer within the - unmentioned - restrictions of a society behind closed walls. The subjunctive form in the final line seems once more to put an element of doubt on the optimistic conclusion. Even if not intended by Wolf in 1961, it begs the question: how long can this situation last? How long are people content with the ordinary humdrum activities of life?

If Christa Wolf modelled prologue and epilogue to her story on Anna Seghers' *Das siebte Kreuz*, she did so from a very different position and the effect is therefore less convincing. Seghers uses the "we" to stress that, even under an evil dictatorship, there are people who are prepared to risk their lives in resisting those in power, and through their example give others strength to survive. Christa Wolf had to persuade her readership that it took courage to live under ordinary conditions, without the need for heroic struggles against adverse powers.

CHAPTER THREE

THE CENTRAL CHARACTERS AND THEIR CONFLICTS

a) Portrayal of the Protagonist: Rita

As we know from Christa Wolf's own account of her difficulties during the initial stages of writing, she laid great store by experience as a basis for writing. Her literary characters were not a mouthpiece for political and social experience, as could so easily have happened in the climate of cultural policies surrounding the writing of the book; some of them, in particular the central character, Rita, took on a life of their own as individuals with human emotions in the process of the narrative. It is therefore of particular importance to the reader to understand the background and motivation of the characters Christa Wolf created and follow their interaction and the way they influence each other. The book abounds in human conflicts and major and minor tragedies, in spite of its underlying affirmation of an optimistic belief in the strength of humanity as a whole. It is clear that the author has difficulties in reconciling the contradiction between, on the one hand, her optimistic and idealistic belief in the goodness of human nature and the ability to reach its goals, if motivated by the right forces, and on the other hand, her realistic experiences of the problems and defeats arising out of the everyday situations. These latter difficulties are, without doubt, greatly aggravated by the political and social circumstances in the GDR of the late 1950s and early 1960s.

It is not without reason that Christa Wolf places her female character, Rita, at the centre of so many conflicting human interests and struggles. Her strength is, to no small degree, based on Wolf's own moral and idealistic outlook. Rita's sensitivity ("Empfindlichkeit"), her joy in life, her optimism and her anxieties are emotions which Wolf could describe from within. Nevertheless, in contrast to all Wolf's female characters in her subsequent works, Rita is not a literary configuration of Christa. She belongs to a different generation: born in 1940, she is not directly affected by experiences during National Socialism - her only memories are those of being a refugee - and she therefore comes to Socialism with a fresh and impressionable mind. It is Manfred, ten years her senior, who belongs to Wolf's generation and lives through the daunting generation conflict, rejecting both parents who represent the unresolved relationship to the past.

In the course of the story, Rita, who has led a simple, secluded, sheltered and dull life as a clerkess in a small town, protected by mother and aunt in their village home, gradually becomes absorbed by the "Sog einer großen geschichtlichen Bewegung". (181) She becomes involved in the social struggles of the GDR at a time of deep political crisis within the country as well as on the wider political stage. Not only her relationship with Manfred, but also her experiences in the factory and as a teacher trainee are described by the author as tests of her inner strength and the endurance of her belief. The subtler shades of her struggles are revealed through her self-doubts, culminating in the crisis which leads her to the verge of committing suicide. Her recovery is seen as a mental process of searching more deeply for the reasons and motivations behind people's actions and words. This process includes self-reflection, to be undertaken by her alone, in almost complete isolation from the outside world. Those who visit her during this period, her former tutors Metternagel and Schwarzenbach, her fellow students and friends, are important only in providing her with a measure of the progress she has made in her self-understanding. This process of healing is of her own doing, with the encouragement of all those who want her to recover. Only Rita can decide when the moment is right for her to leave the shelter and take up the daily struggle in the outside world again. The medical staff at the hospital where she wakes up from her state of unconsciousness, after the accident in the factory, had been too quick in declaring her fit and well ("Sie sind gesund", [9]), but are helpless and uncomprehending when she withdraws into her grief.

The reader too, faced with the contradiction between a love that survives separation and leads to a crisis, and the will and determination to find the reasons which make the separation inevitable, has to show patience and understanding as Rita comes to herself again. Guided by Rita's analysis of her life story, from her first encounter with Manfred to the point of acceptance that they have lost each other despite the strength of their feelings for one another, the reader arives at a deeper understanding of the central character. The author herself very rarely gives her own comments, but leaves it to the reader to read between the lines of the character's own words and thoughts. One particularly intriguing example is a dialogue between Rita and her mentor Schwarzenbach, when the latter visits her at the convalescent home, shortly before she is ready to leave. (181) Asked by Schwarzenbach why she had not followed Manfred to the West, her answer seems

evasive:

> "Vor einem Jahr wäre ich mit Manfred gegangen, wohin er wollte. Heute ..."
> Das ist es, was Schwarzenbach wissen will. "Heute?" fragt er gespannt.
> Rita überlegt. "Der Sonntag nach meinem Besuch bei Manfred war der dreizehnte August", sagt sie, ohne direkt auf Schwarzenbachs Frage zu antworten. "Früh, als ich die ersten Nachrichten gehört hatte, ging ich ins Werk. ..."
> ...
> "Liebten Sie ihn nicht?" fragte Erwin Schwarzenbach. "Haben nicht viele Mädchen blindlings nur danach gefragt? Warum nicht auch Sie?"
> Als ob ich es nicht versucht hätte! Wie viele Nächte habe ich wach gelegen und versuchsweise "dort" an seiner Seite gelebt, wie viele Tage habe ich mich gequält. Aber die Fremde ist mir fremd geblieben, und dies alles hier heiß und nah.

Rita's experience of "die Fremde" should not be taken literally, being restricted, as it is, to one short day in West Berlin; her words are an indication of her own inner state of mind, referring to the process of self-alienation she has undergone in trying to adapt to Manfred's attitude and outlook and all it stands for: his past, his parents, his work environment. The reader recalls that almost her first words to Manfred took the form of the fateful question : "Ist es schwer, so zu werden, wie Sie sind?", (12) implying that to become like him would mean to be alienated from herself. Yet, with this question, Rita first found a way of breaking through the protective wall of cool remote cynicism with which Manfred had surrounded himself. It leads him to ask her the crucial question, albeit "gelangweilt und spöttisch": "Könnten Sie sich in einen wie mich verlieben?", to which Rita gives her impulsive, unpremeditated answer committing herself to him: "Ja". At this point, the narrator adds her own comment to the change which Rita experiences at that moment :"Sie hatte keine Angst mehr, nicht die mindeste." (12)

Her "Angst" returns at crucial moments in the development over the next two years, always at points when Rita feels out of her depth, unable to understand her environment and people's involvement in self-destructive conflicts. Significantly, in the final paragraph of the book the earlier sentence is repeated: "Aber sie hat keine Angst". (199) This time, Rita speaks as an adult, with all the knowledge of a deep and dangerous crisis behind her. The author adds her comment in a final sentence, implying that Rita's recovery has been achieved not through fulfilment as an individual, but through a feeling of trust in her society:

> Das wiegt alles auf: Daß wir uns gewöhnen, ruhig zu schlafen. Daß wir aus dem vollen leben, als gäbe es übergenug von diesem seltsamen Stoff Leben. Als könnte er nie zu Ende gehen. (199)

In between the first moment when she has found fulfilment as a young girl and the final stage when she is integrated into society as an adult, there are many points in which her "Angst" returns: most forcibly when she lies in hospital, reliving the moment she found herself on the railway line between the two fast approaching carriages :

> Sie sagt niemandem, daß sie Angst hat, die Augen zuzumachen. Sie sieht immer noch die beiden Waggons, grün und schwarz und sehr groß. Wenn die angeschoben sind, laufen sie auf den Schienen weiter, das ist ein Gesetz, und dazu sind sie gemacht. Sie funktionieren. Und wo sie sich treffen werden, da liegt sie. Da liege ich. (10)

This passage brings together a number of aspects which are central to the story. As an opening, it adds an element of suspense to an otherwise "banal" love story. Science and technology are seen to be functioning in a way which takes no account of humans - indeed, they can become a threat to the individual's life. It cannot be stressed enough that this was a very controversial and courageous view for a young writer like Christa Wolf at the beginning of her career; it challenges the socialist concept that the future of humanity is based on scientific progress and technical advances.

The strength of the book, which makes it compelling reading even for the present-day reader, lies to a considerable extent in the way in which Christa Wolf conveys to us the development of her central character. Rita, as she is presented to us at the beginning of her relationship with Manfred, is a naive, unsophisticated character who does not reflect, but speaks and acts impulsively, as if guided by a lucky charm. This is what Manfred loves in her when he says "Du kannst zaubern, mein braunes Fräulein". While Rita remains spontaneous, letting herself be guided by her emotions and instincts, she gains influence over Manfred in helping him to take a more positive attitude to life. In the early stages of their relationship, she almost restores in him hope in the future. As she becomes more aware of her environment and more self-conscious, she gradually loses this power.

With every step she takes towards a more adult life, Manfred's faith in her and his trust in himself decreases, to the point where they become almost strangers. His departure to the West catches her completely unawares. Only in retrospect, separated from him for ever, can she see

their relationship in a different light. As she begins to understand the changes she herself has undergone, through her work, her moments of joy and disappointment, even despair, she is able to read the signs of estrangement between herself and Manfred which began long before he leaves. In the end, she accepts herself as a person in her own right who does not give up her own ideals by throwing in her lot with the man she loves. Reading the story from the end therefore presents us with an independent young woman who lets reason rule her feelings, but who nevertheless retains her strong emotions. Rita does not belittle the magnitude of the emotional crisis which followed her separation from Manfred. What held them together was the strength of her emotions; what makes separation possible and bearable is her new ability to rationalize: "Wenn ich mit ihm ginge, dachte Rita, schadete ich nicht nur mir selbst. Ich schadete auch ihm, und ihm am meisten." (181)

This is once again a point where the readers must draw their own conclusions, unaided by conclusive reasons being spelled out by the author. Suspense of disbelief takes on a new meaning. Caught up in the intensity of feeling between Manfred and Rita, which is still present during their last encounter in West Berlin, the reader is asked to find a bridge to the sober, mature character at the end of the book. It becomes apparent that the closing of the border shortly after Rita's visit to Berlin is a mere accident, not the reason behind their separation. Rita and Manfred have not shared the same "heaven" for a long time, whatever this heaven might have represented. Christa Wolf puts a great deal of trust in the strength of those characters who take on the struggle for what seemed to her then, and for a long time afterwards, the best of all possible worlds. The imperfections of this world, human weaknesses and material shortcomings were laid open in the book as a challenge which would bring out the best in people, even if it destroyed them as individuals.

b) Manfred and Rita: the generation gap

In spite of the fact that the story is told mainly from Rita's point of view and through the filter of her reflections and memories, the readers' attention is strongly drawn towards the character of Manfred due to Rita's sustained attempts to understand the reasons and motivations behind Manfred's behaviour and actions. From the early stages of their relationship he is described by her as wearing a mask; the expression on his face is indifferent and ironic ("gelangweilt und spöttisch" [12]), his behaviour as arrogance ("Hochmut" [12]). Rita perceives him as playing

a deliberate role; her question which marks the start of their relationship is designed to challenge this role, to make him step out of it and see it as something he has chosen to become: “Ist das schwer, so zu werden, wie Sie sind?” (12) In his reply “Könnten Sie sich in einen wie mich verlieben?” (12) he continues the role-play, referring to himself as a type rather than as an individual, and likewise, his affectionate nickname for Rita puts her into the role of the nut-brown maiden, reminiscent of German folksongs (“Mein braunes Fräulein” [19]). At their first encounter as a couple, having so far only courted by letter, Manfred talks to Rita in the third person, comparing her to a character in a Russian novel (“Das braune Fräulein mit brauner Pelzmütze. Wie in einem russischen Roman” [15]), and Rita is quick to suggests that they play their pre-set parts as “hero” and “heroine” in a novel to help them over their awkwardness. She is rewarded by Manfred's praise and his willingness to enter into the role assigned to him in the plot she creates for both of them. In this dialogue, Rita and Manfred do not face each other, but address the mirror images in the shop window. (15-16)

Rita's references to “Held”, “Heldin” and “Handlung” in a novel, (“Wir lassen den Roman einfach ablaufen” [15]) represent a form of self-irony used by the author. Christa Wolf here makes oblique reference to features of the traditional novel as adapted by Socialist Realism. This demanded that fiction should be a mirror of reality reflected through the political and social consciousness of the author. The irony lies in the fact far from being politically conscious at this stage, this young couple fits easily into the roles of a trivial romance. The author is aware that this role-play cannot be sustained for long, as reality has to set in. This happens as soon as they enter Rita's home for the Christmas celebrations. Rita's mother and her aunt instantly approve of Manfred as Rita's suitor, whom they find serious, masculine, if a little old for her. (16) But they soon discover the first crack in Manfred's mask during Christmas dinner: when Rita's aunt innocently proposes a toast to his parents, he reacts in both an offended and offensive manner, by telling them of his dream in which he expressed his rage against his father by smashing the family china. (17) Here, as on many real occasions when Manfred clashes with his parents, he abruptly leaves the scene, leaving Rita on her own to cope with the aftermath. On this first occasion, unaware of the reasons behind his outburst, she criticises him, “Du bist ungerecht”, thereby provoking a reaction which reveals the depth of the rift between himself and his father, as representative of the parent generation:

> Läßt er mich in Ruhe, laß ich ihn auch. Zutrinken darf er mir nicht mal im Traum. Warum wollen sie nicht wahrhaben, daß wir alle ohne Eltern aufgewachsen sind? (17)

The "we" here does not include Rita, but refers specifically to what Manfred later describes in an argument with Wendland, his contemporary, as the "gebrochene Generation". (142)

Manfred's anger which is directed both at his parents, who represent the small-minded middle-class society, and at the dogmatic narrow-mindedness of the Party, frequently pushes him to the brink of self-destruction, putting a strain on the relationship with Rita by forcing her to be a witness. At the nightly sessions at the Herrfurth dinner table Rita sees herself as the silent spectator in front of a stage, watching, but not comprehending the play with its loaded silences and violent outbursts:

> Als Zuschauer saß sie vor einer Bühne mit wechselnder Beleuchtung und Szenerie ... ein Schauspiel ... hinter dessen Sinn sie alleine kommen sollte. (33)

She compares this with the "boiling unrest" in the factory where she spends her working days, which she begins to understand and of which she feels part while remaining an outsider to the Herrfurth family. Her way of dealing with the suppressed emotions and outbursts between Manfred and his parents is to be silent and wait for Manfred to explain himself to her. But when this moment comes, she is afraid of what he will reveal to her, and Manfred also doubts her ability to understand his deep-seated rage. (40-41) He disappears for several hours returning late at night to Rita who, fearing that she might lose him, asks to be taken into his confidence, although she knows that this puts the burden of responsibility on her shoulders:

> "Na", sagte er. "Heute hättest du allein schlafen sollen."
> Sie schüttelte den Kopf. "Das nächste Mal nimm mich mit", sagte sie.
> Er sah sie kurz an. "Ich weiß nicht, ob ich dich mitnehmen soll. Ich weiß wirklich nicht."
> Er lehnte an dem rauhen Pfeiler des Gartentors, und Rita konnte keinen Schritt auf ihn zugehen. ...
> Immer werde ich es sein, die ihn halten muß, dachte sie. (40)

Manfred holds Rita responsible for stirring up the past which he had for so long hidden behind resentful silence. But as he prepares to speak, Rita wishes that he would remain silent, afraid of his confession which she is not ready to receive and to which she feels unable to respond. It is

only in retrospect that it becomes clear to her that this was her only chance to hear Manfred speak the truth, normally hidden behind his mask, in an attempt to share his burden with her, even at the risk of losing face:

> Er kam schwer über den Anfang hinaus. So schweig doch! hätte sie am liebsten gesagt. Ging es denn an, daß er ihr berichtete wie einem, dem man Rechenschaft schuldet?
> Oder vielleicht schuldete er ihr Rechenschaft?
> Vielleicht sollte gerade ich ihn damals lossprechen? denkt sie, weil sie doch nicht anders kann, als immer und immer darüber nachzudenken. (41)

What Rita is about to hear from Manfred is an account of his childhood and youth; far from the plain "truth", his story is a mixture of fairy-tale and twisted reality, with frequent references to role-play and disguise. (Chapter 9) He points an accusing finger at his petty-bourgeois parents who brought up their only child in an atmosphere of false expectations and emotions, of lies and deceits. Born in the late 1920s, Manfred's childhood and adolescence coincided with the years of National Socialism. His father, a World War I veteran, joined the Party as one of their minions, "ein kleiner Mitläufer", to compensate for an unhappy marriage to a woman who had aspirations above their station. Manfred was smothered and over-protected by his mother who saw her "destiny" in her only surviving child after several miscarriages. His father treated him either with indifference or with excessive strictness, wanting him to play the role of the obedient son in front of his superior. The father's readiness to switch Party roles in joining the Socialist Unity Party soon after the end of the Nazi era is perceived by Manfred as shameful opportunism which loses him any remaining respect. The mother's burning ambition, her false sense of class which makes her cling to outmoded bourgeois values alienates her from both son and husband and makes her one of the most reactionary, unsympathetic characters in the book. Her ambition for Manfred to become an actor is presented as wish-fulfilment of her own frustrated dreams and, as such, as another form of role-play. Manfred's decision to study science is more a protest against his parents than a declaration for the new era.

But Manfred does not put all responsibility on the parents, he also accuses himself of being caught up in deceit and false role-play as a member of a generation who feels twice betrayed, both by the Nazi movement and by the transition to Socialism. Although Manfred was not technically implicated in any Nazi crimes, he is well aware that his acquiescence in the Hitler Youth could have been easily abused under

pressure.

> In der Hitlerjugend fehlte ich nie, obwohl sie mir zuwider war. Ich sprang mit geschlossenen Augen von jeder Mauer, wenn sie es befahlen. Ich hätte ganz andere Sachen gemacht, mir braucht keiner zu erzählen, wie man aus Angst zum Verbrecher wird. Aber sie zogen mich in nichts hinein, ich war nicht ihr Typ. (44)

Having left school and being too young to join the army during the last few months of the war, Manfred roams the streets as part of a gang who take the law into their own hands as they witness the collapse of the old system. After the war they rebel against their teachers and parents with ridicule and contempt, as they witness those who preached National Socialism at them now trying to convert them to Socialism as the best of all systems. Their credibility gone, there are too few people with an untainted record to set a positive example:

> Wir lungerten einen Sommer lang umher und sahen uns genau an, was die Erwachsenen vor unseren Augen in ziemlich kurzer Zeit mit ihrer Rechthaberei und ihrem Besserwissen angestellt hatten. Die sollen uns bloß noch mal kommen! sagten wir. Wir lachten laut, wenn wir die Plakate lasen: Alles wird jetzt anders. Anders? Mit wem denn? Mit diesen selben Leuten? (44-5)

But even as he tells Rita his story, doubts beset Manfred as to whether she, being ten years younger, will be able to understand him since she does not share the experience of his generation:

> Wozu erzähl ich dir das alles? dachte er. Versteht sie überhaupt, was damals los war? Sie war ja noch nicht mal geboren ...
> Komisch: Irgendwo zwischen ihr und mir fängt die neue Generation an. Wie soll sie begreifen, daß man uns alle frühzeitig mit dieser tödlichen Gleichgültigkeit infiziert hat, die man so schwer wieder los wird? (44)

The "innocence" of those born too late to be responsible for National Socialism and its crimes (ironically a claim made for himself by Chancellor Kohl who masterminded Germany's Unification) is one of the unresolved problems carried on through successive post-war generations in both parts of Germany. Manfred's account in *Der geteilte Himmel* suggests that the new regime in the GDR failed to offer guidance and leadership to a particular category of young people who felt betrayed by the parent generation, and who did not meet the right people with enough integrity to set examples and provide role models for them. Manfred considers it his misfortune to be among those who were disillusioned both by their parents and by the new Party. (46) It is to his credit that he does not absolve himself entirely from responsibility; under Rita's influence he recognizes that he did not try hard enough to find his own answers: "Außerdem: Hab ich sie wirklich gesucht? Und ist es so wichtig, sie zu finden, solange man selber ehrlich ist? ... Kann ich's nicht werden, wenn ich wirklich will?" (46)

In the figure of Manfred, Christa Wolf creates a young man who rejects the simple solution of switching from one role to another, and who owns up to the rift in his own biography which he shares with many of his generation. It is only in retrospect that Rita is able to understand the full implication of his confession to her and put it into context. Before the Wall was closed, neither Rita, nor any other character in the story, is able to accept Manfred's truthful confession. This is put forward as one crucial reason for his isolation and despair which leads to his defection:

> Zum ersten Mal fällt ihr auf, daß es in dieser Zeit alle Augenblicke vorkommt, daß einer dem anderen sein Bekenntnis abnehmen und sich ihm gewachsen zeigen muß. Die Luft ist schwer von Bekenntnissen, als hänge jetzt vieles davon ab, daß aus dem Innersten der Menschen Wahrheit an den Tag kommt.
> Sie denkt: Habe ich denn genug anzufangen gewußt mit seiner Wahrheit? (41)

When Rita recounts Manfred's story, the political crisis has passed, the closing of the border has put an end to the steady drain of working people to the West. Wolf is idealistic enough at this stage to assume that those who remained in the GDR can now afford to be more honest and truthful, especially with regard to their own past. She believes in the words of the character of her next book, *Christa T.*: "Wann, wenn nicht jetzt".

In *Der geteilte Himmel* Christa Wolf was one of the first authors in either part of Germany to address the problem of the generation gap. She linked it to the unresolved question of responsibility for the rise of National Socialism and the collapse of Germany and recognized it as a problem not only confined to the West, but also relevant to the Eastern part of Germany. The GDR had from the outset made Anti-Fascism part of its official policy to substantiate its claim that Fascism was eradicated by the new socialist system. Christa Wolf, on the other hand, demonstrates, through Manfred's failure to adjust to the new society in which he cannot find a role for himself, the problems of her own generation. In Rita, she creates a figure of the next generation who did not carry the legacy of the past and was therefore more open and unbiased towards the new system with its hopes and ideals. As Wolf's biography reveals, she belonged to those who had tried to bridge the generation gap. As a student in her early twenties she eagerly and wholeheartedly accepted Marxist philosophy and socialist ideas as a basis for her integration in the emerging GDR. Her subsequent disillusionment as the first cracks began to appear (the uprising of 1953 in the GDR and of 1956 in Hungary) is reflected in her next book, *Nachdenken über Christa T.*.

Although distanced from Christa Wolf's own biography by gender, Manfred's confession pre-empts the central theme of *Kindheitsmuster*, reflected in the question "Wie sind wir so geworden, wie wir heute sind?" But Nelly Jordan's account of the period before and after the end of the war does not reach the same probing depth as Manfred's confession, and there are no other examples in Wolf's work to match Manfred's explicit account of the negative experiences of his age group during the spring and summer of 1945 in the Eastern part of Germany. In *Nachdenken über Christa T.*, almost all characters, in particular the narrator and the central figure Christa T., belong to Manfred's generation, yet their memories of the period between the end of the war and the early years in the GDR are referred to only selectively.

Ironically, thirty years after *Der geteilte Himmel*, Christa Wolf has still not written a major work about the conflicts arising out of the immediate post-1945 period for young people of her age group who grew up between two conflicting systems, although she has talked about the significance of that period for her generation in several interviews. After the fall of the Wall and the subsequent collapse of Socialism in the GDR, Christa Wolf appears to have discovered how important it is to throw light on those particular conflicts, as we shall see in the final chapter of this book.

Der geteilte Himmel is written against the destructive powers of disillusionment and indifference. Rita, unaffected by Manfred's sombre warnings, - "'Mein braunes Fräulein', sagte er, 'du bist leider ein Kind und ich bin leider ein alter Mann. Das wird nicht gut ausgehen mit uns.'" (19) - is assigned the task of combatting Manfred's deathly indifference by rekindling hope. In the first phase of innocent love she never puts a foot wrong. Following her natural instincts, she passes with ease all the tests to which he puts their relationship as if in a fairy-tale. (19) It is not for long that Rita is allowed to remain in this state of fairy-tale innocence and naivety. The day-to-day reality of the town, the bourgeois enclave of the Herrfurth family, the practical work in the factory, and most of all her negative experiences with narrow dogmatic attitudes as a teacher trainee put her faith in her own strength to a severe test. But she refuses to be defeated by Manfred's repeated warnings: "Aber du wirst nicht durchhalten. Ach du mein braunes Fräulein - glaub mir, du kennst das Leben nicht." (22)

The concept of hope, introduced through Rita's outlook, has redeeming powers for Manfred only for as long as he feels in charge of their relationship. Yet, he is unable to sustain his faith when he has to share Rita with society at large. As she begins to have her own experiences and broaden her contacts with the world around her, she becomes less acquiescent and presents him with a challenge to which he cannot respond. This is apparent when the couple attend a ball to celebrate the factory's anniversary. (Chapter 16) As Rita's confidence grows, she begins to be able to test their relationship outside the protective walls of their little room. In her memory, the high point of this relationship is reached during their trip to the country in a newly bought car, after Manfred has passed his exam. On a different narrative level, this coincides with the turning point in Rita's long journey towards convalescence, as she allows painful and happy memories to come to the surface and begins to accept the past:

> Ein Tag steigt vor ihr auf. Ein vollkommener Sommertag in der Mitte des Jahres. Leichthin hatten sie ihn angenommen, weil er wiederholbar schien nach ihrem Ermessen. In der Erinnerung ist er einzig - Lebenshöhepunkt, Gipfel -, und die Kraft, noch einmal so zu steigen, scheint vergangen. (62)

From the autumn of 1961, Rita reflects back to the summer of 1960. In the history of the GDR this was a time of first reassuring signs that Socialism had become a secure everyday reality. In literary terms, it was the phase termed "Ankunft im Alltag". The exhileration of a drive in the country is turned by Rita into a test for Manfred, both of his own spirit of daring and adventure, and of the potential of science and technology, here symbolized by the car. In her perception, the world is open to them, offering a free spirit of adventure, of exploring and conquering the world.

> Mit großer Geschwindigkeit schwammen sie auf eine Brücke zu, die fern auftauchte, größer wurde, näher kam. Ein schmales, steinernes Tor, hinter dem sich die Weite der Welt auftat, und neue Sehnsucht und neue Weite. (63)

The traditional pattern of the relationship of the sexes takes on a whole new dimension: in challenging Manfred to give his best, Rita herself gains a new face, a sense of equality: "Sie war ihm gewachsen!" (63) Yet, she remains firmly within the confines of tradition; there is no war between the sexes, and Rita is convinced that she owes her new face, a reflection of her growing confidence, entirely to Manfred and finds fulfilment here and now: "Sie war erschöpft und glücklich".

Manfred, following a male role model assigned to him by Rita, gains a sense of satisfaction from being in command:

> Manfred saß locker am Steuer. Er zündete sich eine Zigarette an und blies den Rauch aus dem Fenster. Diese Straße, die Brücken, die vorbeischießenden Bäume - er hatte das alles in der Hand. Das war ausprobiert.
> Manfred beugte sich zu Rita und tippte ihr auf die Nase. "Du kannst zaubern, junge Frau", sagte er. (63)

He feels safe enough to concede that Rita is no longer the "braunes Fräulein" of their early role play, but the mature young woman of a more real world despite the use of the familiar phrase attributing to her the power to perform magic. But this expression itself has gained a more mundane meaning in the everyday context: making the unlikely become possible.

A stylistic feature of the scene is a change of perspective from Rita to Manfred, one of very few instances where the reader gains insight into his thoughts, as a rare expression of confidence in Rita's power to help him overcome his indifference and give him a motivation to become involved in the present:

> Das ist kein schwankender Boden mehr, auf dem ich gehe, dachte Manfred. Zum erstenmal betrete ich festes Land. Sie schafft es, sie macht mich im Leben fest ... Wie kann man sich nur an Teilnahmslosigkeit gewöhnen? (64)

Yet the sense that their relationship is secure enough to give him a foothold in everyday reality is immediately called into doubt in Manfred's reference to the ancient myth of Orpheus and Eurydice. Although he reverses the roles and has Eurydice leading Orpheus from the Underworld, the implied warning is that reality puts a severe strain on the redeeming power of love. (64) The magic bond between Manfred and Rita only works while they are self-sufficient, each complementing the other, without recourse to the outside world. But Christa Wolf makes it clear that self-sufficiency carries its own danger, in isolating the couple from the real world, in their case the social reality of past and present. Rita's memories of the outing stretch over the two central chapters (13 and 14), and although they seem secure in their love for each other, there is a marked contrast between the two chapters. There is joy and fun and a sense of hope in Chapter 13, but also tears, as Rita cries over the memory of a balloon she lost as a child. Manfred interprets her tears as yet another sign in her favour, making her stand out among a flock of dark birds as the only white raven. (67) White is the colour of purity and innocence, but set against a dark world, it makes the bearer of the colour conspicuous and vulnerable.

In reading Chapters 13 and 14 together, the deeper causes for the rift leading to the separation of Rita and Manfred become apparent, as Manfred's need for self-delusion contrasts sharply with Rita's sense of reality and truthfulness. Chapter 14 deals with the remainder of the day with its much more real, yet darker mood, in contrast to the fairy-tale atmosphere of the earlier part. It is overshadowed by the chance meeting between Manfred, Ernst Wendland and Rudi Schwabe. For Manfred, the two men act as a reminder of events in his more recent past as a student, bringing back painful and unresolved memories. A first cautious probing into these events gives rise to a political argument in which Manfred reverts to his role as the disillusioned pessimist who bears grudges. (68-70) From this point on, Wendland features as Manfred's counterpart and rival for Rita's love in the story, as will be discussed in more detail below.

c) Manfred, Rita and Martin: the battle of ideals.

Manfred and Rita's relationship does not withstand the transition from fairy-tale to hard, sober reality. In Rita's account this is sometimes marked by the change from a style that relies heavily on metaphor and imagery and is not always free of trivializing clichés, to a more factual language which describes a situation in black-and-white terms. But the transition is gradual, and the edge is taken off the contrasts as reflection and introspection play a part in Rita's account. The day in the country remains in Rita's memory as a moment of complete happiness, full of hope and confidence in a future with Manfred. Her experience is described as a mixture of a child's dream come true and the first mature relationship of a young adult:

> Alles kann immer wieder neu anfangen, dachte Rita, immer wieder mit ihm. Nun kannten sie sich gerade so viel, um einander sicher zu sein, und gerade

> so wenig, um sich immer wieder zu überraschen. Sogar die kleine Vertraulichkeit mit Wendland, die Rita für sich behielt, brachte sie Manfred näher. (71)

The fairy-tale chapter ends appropriately at midnight, with Manfred suprising Rita with a bunch of carnations to celebrate "someone's 20s birthday". (72) Prior to this, during their homeward journey from the country towards the industrial townscape, the evening sky is divided into day and night, a symbol of the division they are soon to experience in their lives. It is Rita who notices the sharp contrasts created by the moon light, which is at one and the same time soft and dreamlike and harsh and sobering:

> Auf einmal tauchte zu ihrer Linken, genau an der Grenzlinie zwischen Himmel und Erde, eine Lichterinsel auf.
> Sie schwammen schnell darauf zu. Bald unterschied man verschiedene Farben und Stärke der Lichter ... Dann hoben sich schwarze Schornsteinschatten vom helleren Himmel ab. Gestank schlug herein, sie mußten die Fenster schließen. Sie waren wieder im Bann der großen Betriebe. (72)

The author endeavours to give the sober and bleak industrial landscape a romantic appeal which can compete with the romance between the lovers and, indeed, enhance it. This reflects the true spirit of the Bitterfelder Weg where the industrial landscape stands for future hope and as such must hold a stronger attraction for Rita than the idyllic situation which she has experienced during their outing. Ideally, both should complement each other. But how quickly hope can be turned into its opposite is demonstrated by a similar scene, that of their final meeting in West Berlin. (Chapter 29) The striking similarities in the use of metaphors serve as an indication that their separation had begun long before Manfred moved to the West. In comparing the two scenes, the reader becomes aware how far the two lovers have moved apart and how inevitable their separation has become. The encounter in Berlin forms the penultimate chapter of the book and with it, Rita's narrative reflections on the past come to an end.

As Rita and Manfred leave the cafe late at night after a meal and wine (paid for with Manfred's newly earned money in the West), they find themselves alone and isolated in the middle of the city in which they are strangers. Casting their eyes to the sky above, they once again observe a dividing line, between day and night, with the earth - the ground on which they stand - moving fast towards the night. (186-7) The strange, almost surreal, colours of this sky contrast sharply with the black-and-white colours of the divide, suggesting a last desparate attempt to create an illusion against the background of reality. But their subsequent dialogue betrays that it is Manfred who still clings to a dream, while Rita has lost her innocent faith, realizing before him that their separation is real and permanent.

> Früher suchten sich Liebespaare vor der Trennung einen Stern, an dem sich abends ihre Blicke treffen konnten. Was sollen wir uns suchen?
> "Den Himmel wenigstens können sie nicht zerteilen", sagte Manfred spöttisch.
> Den Himmel? Dieses ganze Gewölbe von Hoffnung und Sehnsucht, von Liebe und Trauer? "Doch", sagte sie leise. "Der Himmel teilt sich zuallererst." (187)

This is the moment at which both understand that Rita will not follow Manfred, although their emotions seem to speak a different language: "Ihnen blieb nur dieser schwerelose, blasse, nicht mehr von Hoffnung und noch nicht von Verzweiflung gefärbte Augenblick." (187) The scene and its language contrasts sharply with Rita's memory of their first walk as a couple through the snow in her village: "Wann war es noch mal so? Die beiden Hälften der Erde paßten ganz genau ineinander, und auf der Nahtstelle spazierten sie, als wäre es nichts." (16)

With the metaphorical references to divisions between heaven and earth, day and night, both Rita and the author avoid explicit political comment. Yet, Rita's perception of the situation during her visit to Berlin could not be more realistic. In contrast to Manfred, she recognizes that the magic spell which bound them together has lost its power, and that their separation has become inevitable. The title of the story, "Der geteilte Himmel", thus cannot merely be read as a reference to the Wall which only puts the final seal on their separation.

Social isolation is seen to be a major cause leading to the breakdown in their relationship. There are many scenes in the book which show the couple isolated from their social environment and which are interpreted by Rita in retrospect as danger signals. The most obvious one is their self-imposed refuge in Manfred's room high under the roof of his parents' house, the setting for their idyllic role-play as a couple in the early stages of their relationship. It is here that they experience complete emotional and sexual fulfilment, only hinted at metaphorically, since explicit sex scenes would have offended the censors, if not also Christa Wolf's own moral code. Increasingly, this room becomes a refuge from the real problems besetting their lives, and it is here that

Rita faces loneliness and despair on her own after Manfred has left. The room stands for the dangers inherent in social isolation, and dispells the illusion that two individuals who love each other can be self-sufficient. This age-old theme in literature (Shakespeare's *Romeo and Juliet*, Goethe's *Werther*) takes on a new meaning under Socialism. The precarious nature of a relationship which relies entirely on the other person is evident even where Rita and Manfred seem most secure with each other, shut away from the outside world in their attic room. The more Rita becomes involved in the problems of the factory and matures with it, the more often Manfred needs to be reassured of her love: "Er mußte sich ihrer immer neu versichern." (79)

When, in true fairy-tale style, Manfred asks Rita what she would chose if granted a wish, her reply betrays her own sense of insecurity as two isolated human beings:

> "Immer das gleiche", sagte Rita. "Eine einzige Haut um uns, einen Atem für uns beide."
> "Ja", sagte er. "Aber ist es nicht so?"
> Sie nickte. Es war so, solange die Sehnsucht danach sie nicht verließ. (80)

In her memory, this dialogue is followed by Manfred's nightmare of which he tells Rita:

> "Ich hab geträumt", sagte Manfred, "wir beide sitzen in einem kleinen nassen Boot und schwimmen durch die Straßen einer Stadt. Es regnet und regnet. Die Straßen sind von Menschen leer, das Wasser steigt unaufhaltsam. Die Kirchen, die Bäume, die Häuser versinken in der Flut. Nur wir beide schaukeln noch auf den Wellen, ganz allein in einem sehr zerbrechlichen Kahn." (80)

Rita correctly interprets the dream as a sign of the dangers in becoming isolated from society. In a sudden impulse she reverses the dream situation, suggesting that they are two people sending rescue signals to the lost boat, from the security of their room. Surprised and relieved, Manfred enters into the spirit of the game, allowing himself to be led by Rita's words, like a child who is being reassured by its mother that bad dreams have no power over reality:

> "So sieht jeder, der in Not ist, unseren Leuchtturm?"
> "Ja", sagte Rita."Jeder sieht ihn, wenn er will."
> "Und keiner wird mehr einsam untergehen?"
> "Nein", sagte sie. "Keiner." (80-81)

Although Manfred shows himself willing to accept the comforting lesson behind the story of the rescue, that in the new society no one needs to be lonely and lost, at the beginning of the following chapter Rita's certainty is undermined and shown to be a mere illusion, by the authorial comment: "Neun Monate später war ihr Boot untergegangen. Sie standen an verschiedenen Ufern. Hatte niemand ihre Zeichen erwidert und ihre Not bemerkt?" (81)

Through the figure of Rita, Wolf expressed her own somewhat naively held belief that under Socialism the self-realization of society embraces that of the individual. In her essay 'Selbstinterview' of 1966, written in anticipation of her next book, Wolf develops her idealistic position in giving greater importance to the individual:

> Es ist ein großer Gedanke, daß der Mensch nicht zur Ruhe kommt, ehe er zu sich selber gefunden hat. Die tiefe Wurzel der Übereinstimmung zwischen echter Literatur und der sozialistischen Gesellschaft sehe ich eben darin: Beide haben das Ziel, dem Menschen zu seiner Selbstverwirklichung zu verhelfen. Die Literatur nimmt sich, wie unsere Gesellschaft, gerade der Unruhigen an. Menschen darzustellen, denen diese Unruhe fremd ist: Selbstzufriedene, Platte, allzu Anpassungsfähige - das erscheint mir langweiliger und unergiebiger. (*Die Dimension des Autors*, Vol. 1, 33)

Christa Wolf's own doubts in the wisdom of Socialism are reflected in the figure of Manfred. As a scientist, he represents the future hope of mankind. Yet, it is precisely his devotion to his work which makes him vulnerable as an individual and brings him into conflict with the inflexible norms of the Party. This is further emphasized through the contrast between Manfred and his younger colleague and pupil, who is appropriately named Martin Jung. Martin, who is introduced into the story at a relatively late stage, (Chapter 17) brings a breath of fresh air into the couple's self-imposed social isolation, as the only person whom Manfred calls his friend. He visits the couple in their room under the roof and brings laughter, modern jazz music and a stimulus into their seclusion. (92)

It is Manfred who, overcoming his jealousy and shunning of social contact, introduces Martin to Rita in an attempt to help her out of the crisis brought about by narrow vindictive orthodox attitudes at the teacher-training college. (91) Martin's scientific research arises from his practical work as engineer in an chemical fibre factory, and Manfred, as supervisor of his thesis, becomes involved in the practice as well:

> Er sah sich selbst gezwungen, sich mit der praktischen Arbeit der 'Spinn-Jenny' zu beschäftigen, die Jung verbessern wollte: eine Maschine, über die

> er entzückt und zornig sein konnte wie über eine Freundin. (91)

Martin brings openness and trust into their lives, he is a friend to both of them, the only one with whom Rita can share her concerns about Manfred. Manfred, in turn, can love and admire Martin who, being five years younger than himself, represents the hopes and aspirations for the future of science which he himself has relinquished. He sees this as a stroke of luck which Rita has brought him. (92) But the magic spell has been broken and cannot be regained. Once again Manfred's illusions render him more vulnerable when the harsh reality sets in. His friendship with Martin, and the involvement with the innovations to the "Spinn-Jenny", only lead to disappointment and disillusionment. While Martin's fighting spirit is undaunted, Manfred takes it as a personal defeat when their joint project is rejected. To him it serves as the final proof that his society has no use for him and he becomes resigned and bitter:

> Auf einmal kam ihm vor, er habe insgeheim ein Orakel an diese Arbeit geknüpft: Gelingt sie, wird alles gelingen; mißlingt sie, dann glückt mir überhaupt nichts mehr. Ein freundliches Orakel, solange am Gelingen nicht zu zweifeln war. Nun zeigte es sein schreckliches Gesicht. (110)

But it is not only Manfred's pessimism which makes the rejection of the "Spinn-Jenny" seem a devastating blow dealt to two promising young scientists' work. The policy of stifling and punishing individual initative through decrees from above, often with tragic personal consequences, was one of the most blatant errors of the socialist system. It was based not only on narrow bureaucratic dogmatism, but also frequently on personal intrigue, as in this case. Decisions of the kind which Martin and Manfred experienced were often reversed a few years later, and cases in which those condemned to demotion, even imprisonment, were rehabilitated became more frequent after the closing of the border to the West.

If Manfred and Martin are seen as victims of dogmatism and intrigue at the height of the Cold War climate before the Wall, Christa Wolf goes to great lengths to demonstrate through the contrast in their reaction to the set-back, that these measures were not in themselves a reason for giving up hope in the future of the new society. Martin, who seems to have in him the fighting spirit of his namesake Martin Luther, tries to persuade Manfred to fight for the project with the powers in authority, out of a firm sense of righteousness:

> Ein anderes Projekt, das aus dem Betrieb kam und deutliche Zeichen von Unreife trug, sollte dem ihren vorgezogen werden. Es gab da merkwürdige Dinge. "Wir müssen hinfahren. Aber es wird dann Krach geben." (110)

The consequences of this step seem to vindicate Manfred's pessimism and confirm his worst fears, as Martin is sent down from the University for nine months. While Martin accepts this with philosophical calm, refusing to be defeated, Manfred is doubly hurt by seeing his pupil humiliated. He becomes resigned to the idea that his country has no further use for him and feels free to leave, even at the risk that this might lose him his only two friends, Rita and Martin. Christa Wolf allows Rita to conclude, after her long and hard attempt to come to terms with losing Manfred:

> Martin wäre ein guter Freund für ihn gewesen, und ich eine gute Frau. Auf die Dauer, das trau ich mir zu sagen. Er muß es gewußt haben, sonst wäre er nicht so unglücklich aus S. zurückgekommen - schlimmer als abgewiesen: bar jeder Hoffnung auf künftigen Erfolg. (134)

It is a sign of complete resignation that Manfred is more open towards Rita, prepared to drop his mask of cynicism and indifference for which he has no further use. He escapes into illness, retires to bed and reads Heine, thereby imitating the poet's own miserable end in exile in a room in Paris. (135) Rita makes a final effort to correct his views on the relationship between individual and society: '"Heine ist mit seinen guten Deutschen auch nicht fertig geworden', sagte er. 'Umgekehrt', meinte Rita. 'Die Deutschen sind mit ihm nicht fertig geworden.' (135) Rita's optimism now only provokes a patronising smile from Manfred, a final proof to him that they remain separated by the generation gap: "Er lächelte jetzt öfter über sie, wie Erwachsene über Kinder lächeln." (135)

The more Manfred gives way to pessimism and despair, the more important a role does Martin Jung take on in Rita's life, as a positive example of how to deal with personal set-backs, thereby joining the ranks of the characters of Meternagel and Schwarzenbach who will be considered below. Martin relies on patience and hope ("Geduld", "Zuversicht"). He is a cheerful, winning character, and his youthfulness is a sign of his forward-looking spirit, unhampered by memories and resentments, as Rita recognizes: "Einem zuversichtlichen Menschen kann keiner so leicht widerstehen." (118)

Rita even accepts Martin's criticism of Manfred, as an expression of concern and friendship: "Grob ist er. Er weiß nicht, wie man mit

Leuten spricht. Er stößt sie vor den Kopf. Er ist überheblich. - Aber die Maschine ist gut." (119) And Martin is able to dispell Rita's doubts that Manfred will stand up for himself:

> Rita seufzte. "Wissen Sie - auch ein Held ist er nicht gerade ..."
> "Ein Held!" spottete Martin. "Ein Chemiker und ein Ingenieur werden dort gebraucht, keine Helden ..." (119)

The true hero of the scene is Martin who is prepared to fight, quoting Schiller's Don Carlos: "Wir sind angekommen und fordern das Jahrhundert in die Schranken." (120) For Manfred, the will to fight has been destroyed by personal humiliation and rejection. His belief that he, through his work, can contribute to a better society, has finally proved to be an illusion. The result is a new kind of freedom from ideological commitment and moral responsibility :

> Manfred fühlte sich auf eine böse Weise leicht und frei. Jetzt sah er deutlich ... all die Jahre seines bewußten Lebens hatten ihn auf diesen Augenblick vorbereitet. In seinem Innern sprach er sich für jetzt und für die Zukunft von jeder Verantwortung los. Er war drauf und dran gewesen, sich einfangen zu lassen. ... Manfred hatte ein neues Gefühl von Kälte und Unantastbarkeit. (110-11)

The sympathetic portrayal of the character of Martin as both defiant and patient impairs Manfred's credibility, both for Rita and for the reader, as the story draws to its close. It is significant that Manfred tries to justify his defection in a letter to Martin, the only direct communication after he has left for the West. It is Martin who decides that Rita is the true recipient of the apology: *"Mir scheint, Ihnen gebührt der Brief mehr als mir."* (134) In his letter, printed in italics, in the manner of an authentic document, Manfred makes reference to the wider context of the political experiment of an Utopian society in which he can no longer believe. He gives two reasons for his loss of faith. Firstly, he reminds Martin of their hopes for the 1960s, now shattered: *"Glaubst Du immer noch, sie werden als das große Aufatmen der Menschheit in die Geschichte eingehen?"* (133) Secondly, he refers to the most recent *"Moskauer Parteitagsenthüllungen"*, presumably of 1961, with further revelations about Stalin's purges in connection with the land reforms. Both confirm Manfred's conviction that the price paid for society's advancement, the sacrifice of the individual, is unacceptable: *"Was heißt hier Gesellschaftsordnung, wenn der Bodensatz der Geschichte überall das Unglück und die Angst des einzelnen ist ...* " (133)

Earlier angry discussions with Wendland show that Manfred counts himself among those who are exploited and discarded, for the sake of the greater good. His letter is written out of a need to find justice *("Um der Gerechtigkeit willen")* in Martin's eyes. Martin admits, through his comments to Rita, that he is well aware that he and Manfred were fighting against irrational, evil forces: *"Die Widerstände waren heimtückisch, ungreifbar und unüberwindlich."* (134) In the spirit of the Cold War, he apportions blame for this mainly to one traitor who has since defected to the West. (134) Manfred's letter and Martin's comments reveal both the strength and the weakness of the system in which the author still firmly believed at this stage. It takes the strength and the faith of characters like Martin, Luther's brother in spirit, to take on the challenge. The hard reality of the 1960s demanded sacrifices which Manfred as an intelligent and sensitive individual is unable to make. Rita is caught in the middle as is clearly reflected in the images she uses in describing her memory of the accident in which she nearly dies, and which precipitates the crisis and subsequent catharsis :

> Jener Punkt auf den Schienen, wo ich umkippte. Also hat irgendeiner die beiden Waggons noch angehalten, die da von rechts und links auf mich zukamen. Die zielten genau auf mich. Das war das Letzte. (9)

As she receives Manfred's letter, her first spontaneous reaction reveals that her emotional conflict has not been resolved: "Sie muß warten, ehe sie lesen kann ... Verlaß mich jetzt nicht, ach mein Gott, verlaß mich nicht." (132) This is the only time that Rita - presumably a young socialist agnostic - appeals to God for help. Her child-like prayer (reminiscent of Christ's words on the Cross) suggests that she feels alone and foresaken, in need of a father-figure, an authority to guide her. Martin's comments:

> *Das macht mir am meisten zu schaffen, wenn ich an ihn denke: Wenn er hiergeblieben wäre, und sei es durch Zwang: Heute* müßte *er ja versuchen, mit allem fertig zu werden. Heute könnte er ja nicht mehr ausweichen ...*
> (134)

are not designed to restore her peace-of-mind. They take away the possibility of chosing to stay which Rita claims for herself, and of which she has tried, in vain, to convince Manfred.

d) Ideological Conflicts: Wendland and Manfred (I)

The author's original plan, as outlined in *Dienstag, der 27.September*, was to write "eine Dreiecksgeschichte". In *Der geteilte Himmel*, Wendland, Manfred and Rita do not form a conventional love triangle, but despite Rita's loyalty to Manfred, there is an increasing sense of rivalry between the two male characters as they move further and further apart in their political views. And although Wendland is not a serious contender for Rita's love, Rita discovers in looking back that Wendland had an important part to play in her gradual estrangement from Manfred.

Almost exactly in the middle of the book, Rita gives an account of her dream which tells what she has not yet acknowledged to herself, namely that Wendland is the strong, reliable partner she needs at her side, to stand up to the harsh conditions of life in the GDR. (98) The setting is the sanatorium, the time the beginning of the autumn of 1961: "Der erste klare, kalte Herbsttag nach einer stürmischen Nacht." The previous night has been particularly threatening, with gales which have kept Rita from sleeping: "In der Nacht heulte und brüllte der Sturm im Park. Von den Telegrafendrähten kam ein drohendes Summen." Rita is wakened late in the morning by the sound of her own voice crying for help: "Gegen zwölf erwachte sie von ihrer eigenen Stimme: Sie schrie 'Hilfe, Hilfe'. Mitten in ihrem grundlosen Schreien brach sie ab." (98)

In a much later work, *Störfall* of 1987, a similar scene is portrayed at the end of the book: the narrator is also wakened by her own crying from a gruesome surreal nightmare, the vision of a post-nuclear age. In *Der geteilte Himmel*, however, the dream is linked to reality and, remembered by Rita, does not entirely justify her cry for help.

> Noch sieht sie diese unheimlich lange Straße, die sie nicht kennt. Doch sie erkennt genau ihre Empfindung, während sie diese Straße hinunterläuft (eine Mischung aus Angst und Neugier) - nicht Manfred neben sich, das ist merkwürdig; sondern Ernst Wendland, der nicht hierher paßt, und über dessen Anwesenheit sie sich sogar im Traum verwundert. Er aber tut ganz natürlich und sagt mehrmals : Mir sollst du verzeihen, ihm aber nicht! Und ehe sie antworten oder fragen kann, sitzen sie schon in Ritas kleiner Mädchenkammer im Häuschen der Tante (sie merkt es zuerst daran, daß die Luft, die durch das offene Fenster hereinkommt, nach Wiesen riecht). Hier sind sie noch niemals zusammen gewesen, und ihre Verwunderung wächst. (98)

Dreams, in particular those occuring between sleeping and wakening

(Rita remarks: "Wichtig wäre ihr, den Morgentraum im Gedächtnis zu behalten ..." [98]), frequently play an important part in Wolf's writing. They are a way of revealing a level of truth which is deeper than the objective reality, and they allow the author to introduce a subjective, experimental dimension into the world of verifiable facts. In just such a state between dreaming and wakening, the narrator reveals the secret of her literary character Christa T., her desire to find herself, to be able to say "I". (*Nachdenken über Christa T.*, Chapter 19) Similarly, in Rita's dream she experiences a state of wonder which she compares to the experience of the child saying "Ich" for the first time, thereby recognizing itself as a separate identity. But her dream suggests that she has become an adult, which is the most important step in finding herself after discovering her self as a child. Altogether, the sequence of dreaming, remembering her childhood and recognizing herself as an adult, is linked to the moment when Rita leaves her illness behind.

> Da erwachte sie und fing schon an, den Traum zu vergessen; vielmehr zog er sich wie ein Hauch vor ihren greifenden Gedanken zurück. Die Verwunderung bleibt. Sie läßt sich nur mit dem Staunen des Kindes vergleichen, das zum ersten Mal denkt: *Ich*. Rita ist ganz erfüllt vom Staunen des Erwachsenen. Es hat keinen Sinn mehr, krank zu sein, und es ist auch nicht mehr nötig. (98 - 9)

Apart from Rita's own interpretation of the dream's significance, we as readers are given the task of searching out its meaning. Clearly, the presence of Ernst Wendland (here addressed by his full name) is significant, and his words are the code which needs to be deciphered: when he tells Rita that she has to forgive him, but not Manfred, he implies that both have wronged her in some way. There is enough evidence in the book that Wendland has fallen in love with Rita and regards Manfred as his rival. Although he does not try to win her away from Manfred, the reader is at least aware of his feelings for her, even where Rita is blind to them in her love for Manfred and naively trusting in her friendship with Wendland. Yet, this is only true at a superficial, non-reflective level. With critical hindsight, Rita remembers a number of encounters between herself, Wendland and Manfred which indicate a much more serious involvement which, had the characters been more open and honest, might have changed the course of events.

This becomes apparent when Rita travels to Berlin, having received Manfred's letter to summon her there. (Chapter 26) Her thoughts go back to the previous evening when she had met Wendland by chance, as they were the last people to leave the factory, and she regrets not having told him about her plan to visit Manfred, accusing herself of being arrogant in trying to solve her problems on her own. (163) Their meeting is fraught with unconfessed truths for her, as she carries Manfred's letter in her pocket, knowing that this may be her last chance to speak to Wendland: "Das wäre der Augenblick gewesen, von dem Brief zu sprechen, den ich in der Tasche trug und nicht für eine Sekunde vergaß. Er wird nie begreifen, daß ich es ihm nicht gesagt habe." (165)

Wendland, too, is guilty of hiding his true feelings for Rita from her; instead, he uses the opportunity to speak openly about his problems in the factory for which he has been reprimanded by the Party. For the first time, he uses the familiar "du", while Rita continues to to use the formal "Sie". In contrast to former meetings between them, an awkward silence arises, as both have something to hide from the other:

> Beide sagten sie nicht, was sie sagen wollten - vor allem nicht im richtigen Ton. Sie fanden keinen neuen Anfang - er, weil er nicht wußte, daß dies vielleicht die letzte Gelegenheit zum Reden war. Sie, weil sie es wußte. Ein paar Sekunden standen sie noch unschlüssig. Dann verabschiedete Wendland sich, und Rita ging hinauf. (165)

The reader wonders at this point whether Rita might have been persuaded to give up her plan to visit Manfred if both she and Wendland had been more open with each other. But the author makes it clear that this is not yet the right moment for a new beginning. Rita is still uncertain about her feelings when meeting Manfred again, hoping perhaps that she might win him back on her terms. Besides, she has yet to undergo the traumatic experience of giving up the person she loved most and then live through the ensuing crisis before she can begin a new life. In hospital, at the depths of her crisis, Wendland (who is not introduced by name at this point of the story) appears briefly at her bedside with a bouquet of roses, but the hospital doctor quickly recognizes that he is not the man responsible for Rita's breakdown, although he suspects that he knows more about Rita than all her other visitors in hospital, including her mother. (10)

At the level of day-to-day reality Wendland is not seen as a serious contender for Rita's love, but rather as a dependable friend who gives her a sense of security. The dream, however, reveals that Rita sees him as someone who takes Manfred's place at her side. Deep down, she recognizes the signs that Wendland is trying to win her from Manfred and that he therefore asks her to forgive him, rather than forgiving Manfred whom he does not want to see at her side again. (Through asides in the text the author indicates that Wendland does regard Manfred as an unworthy partner for Rita whom he would like for himself.) But Rita herself also reveals, through the dream, that subconsciously she is longing for a new relationship. Her surprise at finding Wendland at her side, on the long road into an unknown distance, is mixed with fear and curiosity. Finding herself alone with Wendland in the familiar environment of her aunt's house, in the small room where she grew up as a young girl (the smell of fresh meadow through the window adding a faintly erotic note to an otherwise chaste scene), she accepts the new situation. It fills her with wonder, not guilt, a sign that she is as ready for a new relationship as she was when she first met Manfred as an innocent young girl.

At the level of ordinary reality, the dream is referred to again in a scene which follows later in the retrospective narrative, but chronologically precedes the dream. At Frau Herrfurth's funeral, Wendland walks beside Rita, while Manfred is absent which he later explains with a trip to West Germany. Dream and reality become confused not only in Rita's mind, but also in the actual chronology of the narrative sequence. (159 - 60)

> Ernst Wendland, der Rita mit den Augen gegrüßt hatte, hielt sich an ihrer Seite.
> Das alles ging sie zum Glück nicht viel an ... Nur ein Gedanke machte ihr zu schaffen: Dasselbe, genauso, habe ich doch schon mal erlebt. Diesen Verwesungsgeruch vielleicht nicht. Aber die lange Straße. Ernst Wendland neben mir, wo eigentlich Manfred gehen sollte ...
> Endlich fiel ihr ein: Der Traum. Sie fühlte sich erleichtert. Also träumte sie auch jetzt. Alles ist wie in Wirklichkeit - das ist ja gerade der Trick. Man hat Mühe, dahinterzukommen. Aber wenn man erst weiß : Du träumst, dann ist es natürlich sehr komisch ...
> Nachher, wenn ich wach bin, werde ich lange darüber lachen können.
> (159 - 60)

This scene of "déjà vu" takes place in the interim period after Manfred has left, but before Rita receives his letter. The dream, on the other hand, occurs in the period of convalescence after her visit to Berlin. The dream scene and the real scene are, however, juxtaposed in a way that demonstrates that reality is unbearable while the dream contains future hope. It is therefore another literary device which may, or may not, have been deliberately confused by the author in narrating the sequence of events. The funeral scene bears the mark of a grey and stark reality; in believing that she is dreaming Rita finds some relief from the dreadful burden she carries at that moment and which she cannot share with anybody, for emotional as much as for political reasons. As she lifts her eyes, still smiling, from what she wishes to be a dream, she discovers a swallow high above in the sky, a clear symbol of hope. For the first time since Manfred left her she is able to cry, bitterly and inconsolably. At this moment, Wendland is at her side to walk her back through the labyrinth of the cemetery and in this situation she is able to talk to him:

> Jemand nahm ihren Arm - Ernst Wendland, der sie nicht aus den Augen gelassen hatte - und führte sie wortlos die vielen verschlungenen Wege zurück zum Friedhofstor ... Er ging an ihrer Seite die lange Kastanienallee hinunter, bis Rita soweit ruhig war, daß man reden konnte. (160)

Although Wendland has been informed of Manfred's defection by his father who dissociate himself from the son's step, he does not mention him to Rita, nor does Manfred's absence raise any hopes in him to win Rita for himself. This, more than anything, gains him Rita's trust. (161)

When Rita later talks about the dream itself, she no longer needs it as an escape from an unbearable reality. On the contrary, she emerges from it with a clear mind and a new strength to face up to a more sober reality. The author comments:

> Ein wenig blendet sie das nüchterne, klare Licht - wer sehnte sich nicht manchmal nach den leicht verschwimmenden Konturen der Kindheit? Aber sie hat keinen Hang zum Sentimentalen. Sie wird mit diesem Licht schon fertig werden. (99)

This passage, as well as the three paragraphs which follow, describe Rita's new adult outlook on life which she has gained through facing up to the past and the build-up of the crisis in her relationship with Manfred. It is no coincidence that Wendland is part of a dream about an - as yet unknown - future. The optimistic perspective that results from the dream is established before the story reaches its most daunting stage in the final parting of the two lovers in West Berlin. The dream leads to a kind of rebirth where Rita gains a new sensory perception, shedding some of her illusions, but making her more aware, ready to see the grey and brown shades in life, not just the clear, simple primary colours. (99)

It is precisely into this area of the brown and grey tones, the shades inbetween the clear, childlike world of primary colours, that the character of Wendland fits. His role in the book is, in fact, crucial as a counterpart to Manfred, although not in a conventional love-triangle.

His importance lies in his challenging of Manfred's political outlook and in raising the level of Rita's political consciousness. She discovers sides in him which she misses in Manfred. Her first impression of Wendland as he enters the pub where the brigade celebrates their birthday, is of someone too young and inconspicuous for the new post of production manager. (50) Their second encounter takes place soon after the first, with Manfred at her side. At the door of the Herrfurth's villa they almost crash into a man who is hidden in the doorway, lighting a cigarette. (52) Rita, recognizing him, is confused and embarrassed ("verwirrt grüßte sie ihn"); Wendland lifts his hat, acknowledging her in retrospect as the young girl among the men in the pub. Manfred, too, has a dim sense of having met this man before but cannot as yet place him:

> "Wer war das?" fragte Manfred.
> Rita sagte es ihm.
> "Den kenn ich doch ...", meinte er nachdenklich. (52)

Wendland's sudden disappearance before any introduction can take place gives the scene an air of mystery. In fact, it has the makings of a thriller. Wolf might have borrowed the scene from Carol Reed's film *The Third Man*, based on the novel by Graham Greene, set in post-war occupied Vienna, with the attractive woman (played by the actress Alida Alli) between the "bad" and the "good" male characters who know each other from the past. In a famous scene, set in a dark doorway of a large run-down Viennese bourgeois villa, the black-marketeer on the run (Orson Welles) appears for the first time on screen and is discovered by his former friend and author (Joseph Cotton) who is about to betray him to the police. The last scene of the film is set in a cemetery where the woman, whose lover has been buried, walks straight past the "good" man, who betrayed him, along a long road into the uncertain distance. The film avoids moral judgement, despite appearances which show the "bad" character to be clearly in the wrong. The sympathies of the audience are strongly directed towards the female character who remains loyal to her former lover despite his criminal dealings.

Rita's relationship to the two men in her life has similar shades of black-and-white, and, despite romantic undertones, remains firmly rooted in the reality of the GDR of the early 1960s. After the brief encounter with Wendland, Manfred and Rita learn from Manfred's deeply upset father that Wendland has brought the news that their manager has fled to the West, leaving the factory in a crisis, and that

Wendland himself has been appointed in his place. (52) As Wendland is given a heavy responsibility without the opportunity to gain experience first, his case resembles that of Meternagel's "rückläufige Kaderentwicklung", as we shall see later. But Wendland, as the younger of the two, is seen to be more resourceful, and his attempts to bring about changes in the factory are in line with the prevailing tide, whereas Meternagel has to swim against the current. During a crucial meeting called to find the causes for the crisis Wendland gains the trust of the workers, being well informed and speaking plainly about the shortcomings in the production: already, in Rita's perception, he has grown in stature and authority:

> Ernst Wendland war kein Redner, und ein Redner wäre auch das Letzte gewesen, was hier jetzt gebraucht wurde. Er sagte nüchtern, wie die Lage war : Planrückstand ... Mangel an Material, Mangel an Halbfabrikaten, vor allem Mangel an Arbeitskräften ... "Keiner wird uns helfen", sagte er. "Mit Überstunden haben wir lange genug gearbeitet. Der Ausweg ist: Jeder leistet soviel er kann, ehrlich." (60)

But this speech also acts as a signal for Meternagel to reveal to his colleagues in the brigade his own secret plan how to improve productivity. (61) Wolf adheres to the typical feature of the "Betriebs-roman", as workers and managers are seen to join forces, yet, she deviates from the pattern in that Wendland and Meternagel go their way without recourse to the bureaucratic level and therefore risk being reprimanded by the Party. Their actions are vindicated by their success, as the factory recovers, and, moreover, private grievances between Wendland and Meternagel are laid to rest. Rita experiences this process at first hand, while Manfred remains in self-imposed isolation with his pessimistic, sceptical outlook. His question to Rita when she returns from the meeting in the factory concerning who has been made the scapegoat (using the suggestive term "crucified") for the mistakes, is based on his own deeply negative experiences: "Oder sei es etwa nicht darum gegangen, den Schuldigen zu kreuzigen?" Rita's reply is not an answer, since she is unable to understand what Manfred implies, not having shared his experience. Instead, she continues her own private train of thoughts which makes her see Wendland in a new light: "'Ja', sagte Rita langsam, 'Der Wendland hat gut gesprochen.'" (61)

As Rita finds out more about Wendland's life, her trust in him increases, and as she has frequent opportunity to compare the two men, Manfred comes off worse. Despite very different family background and personal circumstances, Ernst Wendland and Manfred Herrfurth share the experience of the first generation of adult men in the GDR after the war. Yet, Wendland is seen as the more experienced and mature of the two who men. He has already been given responsible offices, both in the Party (when Manfred first met him, Wendland was a district leader of the Free German Youth Movement (FDJ Bezirksleiter), and Rita gets to know him as the new production manager (Produktionsleiter) in "her" factory. As one is set up in a position of authority where the other is not, this leads to conflict between the two characters and brings about confrontation whenever they meet. Manfred bears a grudge against Wendland and others who have acted according to the functions given to them by the Party, long before he meets Rita. This is made clear at the first meeting of the two men at the garden restaurant, during the outing to the country, (already referred to above). As Wendland is introduced to Manfred by Rudi Schwabe, a former schoolmate who has since made a career for himself as FDJ secretary, memories return of an episode in the past which the three men had shared. (68) Wendland, in his position as FDJ Bezirksleiter, had saved Manfred from being expelled from school for his rebellious remarks in the jazz club. Jazz was regarded as subversive by the Party, and those who listened to it were seen as sympathizing with the West. Looking back, Wendland wonders whether his intervention had diffused the political issue instead of bringing it out into the open: "Allerdings weiß ich bis heute nicht, ob die Verhandlung nicht *auch* aufs politische Gleis gehört hätte, wenn auch in einem anderen Sinn ..." These remarks arouse Manfred's resentment and cynicism, an attitude to which he also resort in all subsequent disputes with his rival:

> "Zweifellos", sagte Manfred pikiert. "Zumindest nach der Theorie, daß alles, was ein Mensch sagt, tut, denkt, fühlt, Politik ist. Wir sind nun mal die politische Generation, nicht wahr?"
> Wendland sah ihn prüfend an, blieb aber freundlich. Ganz so weitherzig lege er diese Theorie gar nicht aus, sagte er. (68)

Rita, sensitive to Manfred's irritation without understanding its cause, avoids open conflict by asking Manfred to dance with her, but she cannot brush away his anger, he remains "verstimmt" and "gereizt". At this stage Rita is still secure enough in her feelings and is able to acknowledge Wendland's qualities without threat to her relationship to Manfred: "...ihr gefiel der nüchterne, gründliche Wendland, der so verschieden von Manfred war." (69)

In Rita's mind, the two men are equals, as both have crucial roles in the new society, Manfred the young scientist who has just gained his first academic success, Wendland the man who holds a responsible post in the field of practical work; in an ideal situation, they could be expected to work together towards the same goal of improved social and economic conditions. But Wolf does not idealize, rather, she chooses to show the conflict and rift developing between these two characters. The cause is not their rivalry for the same girl, but a much deeper ideological difference. In their arguments Manfred plays the devil's advocate, challenging the belief in dialectical historical materialism on which Socialism is built, thereby pushing Wendland onto the defensive. The incongruity and imbalance of their positions becomes evident: the two men are unable to conduct a dialogue which allows each to argue his point and thus sustain a healthy antagonism. This is made apparent in two encounters: Wendland's visit to Manfred's laboratory, (Chapter 18) and Manfred's participation in the trial run of the new railway carriage, (Chapter 23) as each, rather reluctantly, enters the other's territory. The first scene takes place without Rita being present. As the two young men have an opportunity to take the measure of each other, there appears to be common ground between them. However, the second scene, not long before Manfred's defection to the West, reveals the unbridgeable rift between them.

In Rita's memory, Wendland's unscheduled visit to Manfred's laboratory is preceded by two episodes: by her dream in which Wendland takes Manfred's place, and by one of the rare occasions when Manfred speaks openly to Rita about his philosophical position as a scientist. (99 - 100) From the position of the sceptic in the socialist camp, he claims that, so far, scientific progress has only generated materialism and war, both attributed to Capitalism: "Doch auch die Voraussagen der Elektronengehirne änderten nichts daran, daß auf der Erde (auf einem Teil der Erde, meinetwegen) weiterhin in großem Stil spekuliert, weiterhin in großem Stil gerüstet wird." (100) In response to Rita's timid interjection: "Aber die Menschen?", he is prepared to concede that scientific development can have an impact on the future of humanity in its everyday existence, and that his frustration stems from the fact that progress is too slow:

> Der große Anteil seiner Wissenschaft am zukünftigen Alltagsleben der Menschen befriedigte ihn, und wenn er überhaupt Ungeduld kannte, so war es die Ungeduld des Experimentators, dem nicht schnell genug ganze Städte und Länder als Objekt für seine Experimente zufielen. (100)

In the conversation which follows, between the two men, Wendland shares this impatience, but holds the scientists, not the system, responsible for speeding up the process. "'Beeilt euch damit', sagte Wendland." (100)

The fact that the two men meet first in the laboratory, the place where Manfred's teaching and research take place, is significant in the context of the early 1960s when scientific development and technological advancement were officially declared to be the basis for the future development of Socialism, and progress was measured by the improved quality of life for each of its members. Despite its antagonistic position vis-à-vis Capitalism, Socialism was competing with the visible scientific and material advances achieved in the West, in particular the Federal Republic under Adenauer and his Economics Minister Erhard. In the GDR, during the same period, scientists and production managers in industry alike were hampered in their efforts not only by the lack of a material basis, but also by a narrow-minded bureaucratic Party obsessed with the class struggle.

While Manfred and Wendland can be seen as prototypes of two young, capable and committed men, working for similar aims, each providing what the other needs for progress in his work, they cannot find a level of dialogue to bring them closer. Each is seen as having a blind spot with regard to the other: Manfred resents Wendland's political alignment, and Wendland is irritated by retrogrades and renegades among the scientists who measure their own achievments against those in the West, thereby denying the GDR a sense of progress. In bringing the two characters together, Wolf shows that each needs the other and that they should be seen as fighting side-by-side, not against each other. Manfred is proud to show Wendland his work, and demonstrate to his colleagues that those who run the industry need the scientists:

> Manfred führte ihn zu seinen Kollegen - wie oft wurde einer von einem Werkleiter besucht! - und erläuterte, woran sie arbeiteten. Er zeigte sich etwas enger mit Wendland befreundet, als der erwartet hatte und nutzte den Vorteil, den Gegner einmal auf eigenem Gebiet zu haben. (101)

Wendland measures up the unknown territory of scientific research and is impressed by the sober functionality. He concedes a point to Manfred, yet remains in control, sharing with the reader his secret thoughts. He smiles "offen und entwaffnend", and there is a silent agreement between the two men to bury the hatchet, at least as regards their rivalry for Rita. The author comments, from Wendland's point of view:

> Waffenstillstand. Wer wird so unfair sein, eine momentane Schwäche des Gegners auszunutzen? Was heißt überhaupt Gegner! Wegen des Mädchens? Nun gut. Aber schafft so etwas nicht auch Beziehungen zwischen Männern? Darüber spricht man nicht. (101)

The use of military metaphors by both characters betrays a rivalry which is stronger than jealousy about a woman, although this certainly influences their distrust of each other. That they are in opposite camps becomes apparent when their conversation returns to the role of science for the future of society, with Manfred's veiled comments on progress in the West implying criticism of the GDR. Wendland counters this by bringing the issue out into the open:

> "Nun ja", sagte Manfred dann. "Da Sie mich durchschauen: Meinen Sie nicht, daß anderswo die Wissenschaft schneller in den Alltag eindringt als bei uns?"
> "Westlich der Elbe zum Beispiel", ergänzte Wendland, ohne Vorwurf im Ton.
> "Zum Beispiel", bestätigte Manfred ... Hier, soweit müßten wir auch sein. - "Und warum sind wir's nicht?" - "Fragen Sie die Leute, die dafür verantwortlich sind!" - "Warum fragen Sie sie nicht selbst?" (102)

By tossing the argument to and fro, as children would, neither takes a clear stance. It is striking that Wendland, the convinced Socialist, on this and all subsequent occasions, fails to produce a convincing argument to counter Manfred's scepticism, expecting him merely to accept the superior wisdom of the Party. Not surprisingly, Manfred, who feels he is being treated like a child, reacts with resigned protest: "So sind sie alle. Speisen einen ab. Weiß er denn nicht, was für Antworten unserereiner auf solche Fragen kriegt? Belehrungen, bestenfalls. Kinderbelehrungen." (102) On the surface, this first confrontation ends amicably, but through the implied comment by the hidden author, the reader is made aware that appearances do not reflect the real situation. (102 - 3)

In the more private situation of the restaurant, Wendland speaks openly about his personal problems. On this day, his thirty-second birthday, he has received an official dusting down ("Gardinenpredigt") by the Party for his initiative in getting the material he needed to continue production in the factory. (102 - 3) Manfred shows interest in Wendland's story and feels reassured that he is not being taught a lesson: "Er war nun endgültig überzeugt, daß ihm hier keine Lektion gehalten wurde." (104) Yet, the lesson for Manfred - and the reader - lies in Wendland's way of dealing with personal set-backs and defeats. As far as the greater goal is concerned, there is no contradiction in being both wrong and right, and Wendland puts the Party's point above his own individual pride.

> Sie haben mir den Kopf gewaschen, und ich hab schließlich stillgehalten. Was soll man machen ? Sie haben recht, und ich hab auch recht. So was gibts. (104)

It is worth noting that Meternagel, for his part, comes to the same conclusion after being demoted by the Party for the first time - an indication how closely these two figures are linked in Wolf's concept.

Wendland uses his story to prove to Manfred that Socialism does have an advantage over the West, where a man in his situation would have lost his job, while in the GDR, he gets away with being reprimanded. (104) In this way, by turning personal examples into a lesson, figures like Wendland and Meternagel are seen to win their arguments, without resorting to ideological dogmatism. But it is equally clear that it takes a more subtle argumentation to convince intelligent sceptics like Manfred of the need to sacrifice his personal pride and overcome his deep-seated doubts. Perhaps against her own better judgement, Christa Wolf lays open a crucial weakness in the system.

Before moving on to the second encounter between the two men which ends in bitterness, we should note that through Manfred's detailed account of his encounter with Wendland, Rita begins to know Wendland, and she gains a much more profound insight into the contrast between the two men and the reasons behind their conflict: "Rita erfuhr von keinem anderen Menschen soviel über Wendland als von Manfred, am Abend nach diesem Tag." (103)

e) Wendland and Manfred (2)

The second confrontation between Manfred and Wendland, during the test drive, the "Probefahrt", reveals the unbridgeable rift which separates Manfred from everything that Wendland and Rita believe in. The date is 12 April 1961, the setting the journey through the GDR in the newly constructed railway carriage. (Chapter 23) Rita's presence, her vivid recall of the occasion are stressed by a frequent switch to the first-person narrative. The day becomes a symbolic milestone in the scientific achievement and idiological struggle, with the news, *"Die Nachricht"*, (142 - 3) that the Russians have put the first man into space. In Rita's memory, that day is like a jigsaw puzzle: personal memories are fitted around the extraordinary historical happening. Ordinary everyday normality is constantly measured against the cosmic event. It is in this context that Manfred confronts Wendland, both before and after receiving *"die Nachricht"*, with his deeply pessimistic views, once again doubting the influence of science on the future of humanity. Invited by Wendland to take part in train journey designed to test the performance of the new carriage, Manfred feels isolated, the odd one out among the workers with whom Rita identifies since she has been part of the team who built the carriage:

> Rita teilte die Unruhe und Besorgnis, die, ohne ausgesprochen zu werden, alle ergriff. Was jetzt gesprochen, vereinbart, veranlaßt wurde, war ihr durchschaubar. Hier war etwas, was sie nicht nur obenhin kannte : Diesem Wagen ... sah sie unter die Haut. Sie war froh darüber. Ich gehöre dazu, dachte sie.
> ... Manfred sah Rita lachen und wußte, daß sie jetzt ein Glück empfand, von dem er ausgeschlossen war. Sie sah, daß er das Gesicht verzog und fragte sich erschrocken: Womit hab ich ihn verletzt? (145)

But even before they join the train Manfred and Rita are aware of a beginning estrangement in their relationship as they both realize that they can no longer communicate with each other.

> Sie gingen, noch immer stumm, ein paar Schritte. Da sagte Manfred: "Kann man mit dir nicht mehr sprechen?"
> Rita fühlte sich ertappt und suchte Ausflüchte, aber er sagte leise: "Laß doch. Ich weiß ja."
> "Was weißt du?" fragte sie.
> "Daß ich unerträglich geworden bin. Unerträglich mißtrauisch." (137)

As the journey proceeds the spectrum of ordinary everyday life passes by, an industrial landscape consisting of agriculture, heavy chemical industry (Bitterfeld is close to Halle, which is presumed to be the town where Rita and Manfred live), and open-cast mining which has left deep scars on the land. (140) For Rita, (and Christa Wolf, at that stage), the ecological implications take second place to the human aspect. The view from the window offers Rita reassuring signs of ordinary everyday activities which, to her, guarantee the fabric of life.

> Sie waren beschäftigt, aus Millionen Handgriffen und Worten und Gedanken einen Tag zu machen, einen gewöhnlichen Erdentag, der sich am Abend ohne Aufhebens zu seinesgleichen legen würde, zufrieden mit dem wenigen, was er dem Leben zugefügt hatte: kaum sichtbar, doch unersetzlich. (140)

By complete contrast, Manfred's view through the window leaves him angry and disillusioned as he sees the old, decaying villages passing by. He makes Wendland, who has joined the couple, responsible for the failure of Socialism to change the quality of life:

> "Sehen Sie sich das an", sagte Manfred. Ich hatte kaum bemerkt, daß Wendland schon eine Weile bei uns saß, und mir war auch entgangen, worüber sie redeten; aber es war vor *der Nachricht*, das weiß ich genau; denn später änderte sich der Ton ihrer Gespräche. "Sehen Sie sich das an, als Realist. Aus diesem Material wollen Sie Funken schlagen?"
> "Worauf wollen Sie hinaus?" fragte Wendland.
> "Auf eine Kleinigkeit", erwiderte Manfred. "Auf die Tatsache, daß gewisse Bemühungen für dieses Land zu spät kommen. Historische Verspätung - das sollten wir als Deutsche doch kennen!" (141)

We note that Manfred's aggressive and pessimistic outburst cuts into Rita's daydreams - this gives them added importance, as we have seen when discussing Rita's dream. At first, she remains silent, leaving the arguing to the two men. Manfred's argument is, in fact, an important challenge to the idea that human nature is capable of change and progress - crucial for those who are involved in turning the inhabitants of one part of Germany into a socialist society, persuading them that the cause justifies the means. In contrast to his earlier argument about the lack of progress in science, Manfred here does not point to the comparison with the West (a dangerous example because of the high standard of living reached in a short time), but instead demonstrates why Socialism is not made for the Germans with their legacy of the past. To prove his point, he uses Marxist-Leninist jargon to put forward the views branded as bourgeois reactionary:

> "Sozialismus ist wie geschaffen für die östlichen Völker", sagte er. "Sie können, unverdorben durch Individualismus und höhere Zivilisation, die einfachen Vorzüge der neuen Gesellschaft voll genießen. Für uns führt kein Weg dorthin zurück. - Was ihr braucht, sind ungebrochene Helden. Was ihr hier findet, sind gebrochene Generationen. Ein tragischer Widerspruch. Und ein antagonistischer." (141 - 2)

Antagonistic contradictions and, for that matter, individualism were rejected by Marxist-Leninist ideology which embraced only non-antagonistic conflicts which could, and would, be resolved through historical dialectics. Moreover, in pronouncing the Eastern nations untouched by culture and civilisation Manfred puts forward outmoded romantic views with racist undertones, which, in a different context, could quickly be turned into fascist propaganda. The author presents

Manfred as a victim of an unresolved relationship to the past, unsuited for the new society. He condemns himself when he describes his generation, including Wendland, as a "gebrochene Generation", burdened by a past. As such, they can neither accept the new order naively and spontaneously (like Rita), nor can they be the leading figures in the fight for Socialism, like the heroes of the "Aufbaujahre". With this view, Manfred distances himself (and his contemporaries) from those who were set before them as examples, the first generation of anti-fascist Socialists who were put in charge of re-educating the young generation in East Germany after 1945. In the literature of the 1950s this generation was portrayed as "heroes" of the first hour and as such formed a vital part of Socialist Realist writing. By contrast, Manfred and Wendland belong to Christa Wolf's generation who no longer saw themselves as heroes and did not seek a place for them in literature. This is made explicit in Rita's conversation with Martin which we discussed above. At this stage in her writing, Wolf had to recognize that not all conflicts could be resolved and not all doubts silenced. It is therefore not surprising that Wendland, representing the "ideal" young Socialist, cannot find convincing arguments to counter Manfred's accusations, resorting instead to the feelings of personal rivalry and using bland Party jargon :

> "Viele Irrtümer auf kleinem Raum", sagte Wendland. Es machte ihm keinen besonderen Spaß, diesem Doktor sein Weltbild geradezurücken, den man doch immer wieder sehr ungern neben dem Mädchen sah. Doch er war höflich genug, zu antworten. Manfred verwechsle wohl die herrschenden Klassen der westlichen Völker mit den Völkern selbst. (142)

Manfred has reason to feel that this answer presents no challenge: on the contrary, it confirms his scepticism: "Manfred belächelte geringschätzig dieses Argument, das er erwartet hatte; Wendland, der selbst merkte, daß seiner Entgegnung das Feuer fehlte, wurde ärgerlich." Resorting to literature, with the example of Dr. Faustus, (an indication of the important role assigned by the GDR to its classical heritage, in particular Goethe), Wendland provides Manfred with further ammunition in arguing against the progressive nature of history:

> "Eben", sagte Manfred. "Aber zwischen diesem faustischen Zorn und uns liegen die Jahrhunderte. Das ist, was ich sage."
> Sie schwiegen unlustig.
> Rita sah, daß Rolf Meternagel Manfred schweigend und aufmerksam musterte. (142)

This is one on the numerous examples of silence replacing communication. Those who argue, expressing justified doubt, are ousted by this silence. Neither Wendland nor Meternagel, the nearest figure to a "hero", find or seek a way of addressing Manfred's problem. His "Republikflucht" is the logical conclusion of this process. When it is too late Wendland, looking back to the "Probefahrt", admits to Rita that he made a crucial mistake in omitting to challenge Manfred's point of view, even if it meant risking antagonism. (148) Rita, too, understands in retrospect that she had taken too much for granted and that her integration in the Brigade Ermisch had protected her from facing up to conflict and doubt, preventing her from recognizing how isolated Manfred had become. (145)

The author, in presenting us with different perspectives, allows the readers to draw their own conclusion; there is in fact no way in which Manfred, with his different background and past history, can become integrated in the Brigade and share their ordinary problems. Indeed, all along he warns Rita that she, too, will be defeated by the ordinary insoluble problems of the factory which here stand for ordinary day-to-day living in the GDR. As Brecht had put it in 1949, in one of his later poems: "Die Mühen der Gebirge liegen hinter uns/Vor uns liegen die Mühen der Ebenen". Manfred's attitude and the problems this creates for Rita and other "positive" characters in the book make it apparent that, even at this stage, there was no simple "Bitterfelder Weg" for Christa Wolf.

The experience which is shared by all, the news of the first man in space, leaves Manfred feeling excluded and embittered. But for different reasons Rita, too, feels alone and frightened, unable to share her secret fears and doubts with anyone, and she escapes into silent (inner) monologue :

> Soll sie denn ganz und gar aus den Angeln gehen, deine Welt, die dich doch, was immer sie dir angetan haben mochte, umschloß als einzige Möglichkeit deines Daseins? ... Wirst du der plötzlichen Befreiung vom So-und-nicht-anders gewachsen sein? Wird unser bißchen Menschenwärme ausreichen, der Kälte des Kosmos standzuhalten? (143 - 4)

Rita's doubts concern the ability of human beings to cope with scientific progress without losing sight of their values. For Manfred, putting a man into space is the final proof that scientific development has been abused by those in power, taking advantage of the hard work of ordinary people, but depriving them of the benefits of their troubles, as the whole operation is nothing but a huge propaganda coup against the West. (146 - 147) Once again, no one rises to the challenge of trying to argue with this view which, to the impartial outsider, must appear realistic and justified. From the partisan point of view, with which the author identifies strongly at this stage of her writing, however, it is seen as sheer heresy and deemed unworthy of argument: "Manfred bekam keine Antwort. Wendland schwieg aus Taktgefühl - er konnte sich nie gegen einen sichtlich Schwächeren wehren - Rita aus Scham und Zorn." (146) Rita still wants to believe that there is a real ("idealized") Manfred hiding behind the disguise of the angry petit bourgeois, when she asks silently: "Das bist du doch nicht! Was suchst du in dieser Krämermaske?" With hindsight, Rita finds an explanation for Manfred's behaviour as the disillusionment of someone who sees himself the victim of history: "Heute versteht sie ihn besser: 'Der Bodensatz der Geschichte ist das Unglück des einzelnen.' Er tat damals schon alles, diesen entnervenden Gedanken in sich zu festigen." (146) In allowing Rita to slip into ideological jargon, Christa Wolf avoids focussing on the real reason for Manfred's conflict as an individual in a social and political situation with which he cannot identify:

It is to the credit of the book that the question of whether Manfred is really the sole perpetrator of his misfortune remains unanswered in the reader's mind. Both Manfred and Wendland are seen in a negative light in their confrontation during the "Probefahrt". Wendland takes advantage of Manfred's already weak position, by referring to his father's demotion at work, a fact of which Manfred was not yet aware, and which he sees as a further sign of manipulation of the individual by those in power. He turns the argument into a moral issue, when he accuses Wendland as the representative of the new order of having failed in their attempts to create a human society on the basis of ethical values. When Wendland confirms that this is indeed the precondition on which to build the future of socialist society, Manfred pronounces this hope a mere illusion, a last resort, before admitting the inevitable defeat:

> "Ich bedaure nur die Unmasse von Illusion und Energie, die an Unmögliches verschwendet wird. Moral in diese Welt bringen! - Das wollt ihr doch, nicht wahr?"
> "Es ist eine Existenzfrage für die Menschheit", sagte Wendland.
> "Eben", erwiderte Manfred. "Die letzte Hoffnung. Gescheitert, wie die Dinge einmal liegen. Eines Tages werdet ihr es zugeben müssen." (147)

In finally rising to this challenge, Wendland (like Rita had done, silently) accuses Manfred of wearing a mask, a disguise to hide his true feelings. This earns him Manfred's respect, although only briefly:

> Wendland hatte sich aufgerichtet. Scharf sagte er: "Und wozu brauchen Sie diese Deckung?"
> Rita erschrak, ohne zu verstehen. Manfred verstand, ohne zu erschrecken. Er zeigte Anerkennung für Wendlands Scharfsinn. Dann bediente er sich, verletzend nachlässig, wieder seiner Maske. (147)

The author, clearly concerned that Manfred should be seen as being in the wrong, does not allow him to drop his mask long enough to show his true feelings. The reader may ask at this point whether all three character are not in fact wearing masks, with Manfred being at his most vulnerable, but also his most authentic and truthful, when he is driven to show his true face:

> Manfred drehte sich noch einmal um, ehe er in den Zug einstieg ... er hielt ihnen sein Gesicht hin, erbarmungswürdig nackt ... "Abschminken! Die großen Gefühle, die tönenden Phrasen ... endlich abschminken! Das ist das einzige, was uns bleibt." (148)

In the evening after the test drive, alone in their room, Rita realizes that she has become the only person in Manfred's life whom he still trusts and on whom he depends, and she begins to doubt her ability to fulfill this part. (148) Love, "die großen Gefühle", belong to a literary tradition which Christa Wolf knows through reading the classics, but they no longer suffice in portraying modern relationships in a society where historical and social forces are deemed to have precedence over individual love: without them, relationships are threatened.

The long and unresolved confrontation with Manfred during the "Probefahrt" shows that the author was well aware, not only of the ideological, but also of the psychological difficulties involved in convincing someone that Socialism, against all the odds, presented the future hope for society; putting forward rational arguments convincingly does not come easily or naturally to Rita whose emotions speak a different language. The more she denies herself direct access to these feelings and identifies with the ideological arguments, the less convincing she becomes for Manfred, and for the reader. Unlike his famous ancestor, Faust, Manfred cannot be saved - not even by the eternally feminine, love.

From the vantage point of the present, after the collapse of Socialism in Eastern European countries and in Russia, the clash between Manfred and Wendland, the insoluble nature of their conflict takes on a different significance. Manfred's argument against Socialism - his scepticism with regard to its benefits for humanity, including scientific progress, becomes a self-fulfilling prophecy. It seems no longer surprising that Rita, Wendland and Meternagel cannot convince him of their position. In retrospect, Socialism as portrayed by Christa Wolf in her book is dogmatic and inflexible, and her attempts to distinguish between rigid Party officials on the one hand (Mangold and Schwabe), and those who represent a humane and not infallible form of commitment to Socialism (Schwarzenbach, Wendland, Meternagel), on the other, seems artificial and contrived. Yet, the human appeal of the story is undeniable, due largely to the touching faith of the figure of Rita.

Manfred, on the other hand, has learned his lesson from growing up under two different, but equally authoritarian systems, that man is capable of the worst betrayals. His scepticism and pessimism appears now as much more realistic and authentic than Rita's efforts to stand up for her ideals, based on the belief that society can be bettered, provided the conditions are improved. Despite her apparently probing and critical approach which made the book a lot of enemies at the time, the author leaves taboos untouched - one such taboo being the belief in the inherent rightness of Socialism which needs no justification.

CHAPTER FOUR

"DER SOG EINER GROSSEN GESCHICHTLICHEN BEWEGUNG"

THE PARTY AND THE WORKFORCE

a) The Struggle against Party Dogmatism: Schwarzenbach versus Mangold

The introduction of the theme of factory work, the detailed description of problems encountered and ways of resolving them, and, above all, the involvement of individual characters in this process have a crucial role in the book as a whole. Indeed, it might be argued that Rita's involvement with the Brigade Ermisch has a more lasting influence on her development than her relationship with Manfred and that in the choice between following Manfred or staying in the GDR, it is the commitment to the Brigade which determines her decision. In her attempt to explain to Schwarzenbach why she left Manfred in spite of her love for him (and contrary to the conventional expectations that young women followed the dictates of their heart, which even the good Socialist Schwarzenbach shares), Rita, as we have seen, does answer indirectly by describing her immediate reaction to the news of the closing of the border in Berlin, a few days after her visit in Berlin:

> "Vor einem Jahr wäre ich mit Manfred gegangen, wohin er wollte. Heute ..."
> Das ist es, was Schwarzenbach wissen will. "Heute?" fragt er gespannt. Rita überlegt. "Der Sonntag nach meinem Besuch bei Manfred war der dreizehnte August", sagt sie, ohne direkt auf Schwarzenbachs Frage zu antworten. "Früh, als ich die ersten Nachrichten gehört hatte, ging ich ins Werk. Als ich sah, daß ich nicht die einzige war, wurde mir bewußt, wie ungewöhnlich es war, daß so viele am Sonntag in den Betrieb kommen. Manche waren gerufen worden, andere nicht." (181)

Rita is among those who did not wait to be summoned by the Party, but who followed an inner call to the workplace where she feels most at home. It is significant that she, as a student, does not feel compelled to go to her other work environment, the college. Schwarzenbach, as one of her teachers and spiritual mentor, understands her reaction: "Schwarzenbach weiß, was sie sagen will. Es ist nicht sehr verschieden von dem, was er selbst, was sie alle an jenem Sonntag erlebt haben." (181) The importance of the factory and all it stands for in Rita's development is strongly contrasted with her experiences as a student at the "Lehreranstalt". These latter ones are largely negative, and lead to a crisis where she begins to doubt her decision to become a teacher. Indeed, the strength she has gained through her involvement with the Brigade is eroded by the narrow, vindictive dogmatism at the college. This dogmatism is centered on the figure of Mangold, an older student who has gone through a strict "Parteischule" and who represents everything that Rita does not want to be. To Manfred, she complains: "Man fordert uns die ganze Zeit auf, von Mangold zu lernen. Das kann ich nicht. Ich will's auch nicht. *Muß* man wirklich so werden wie er?" (96) It is significant that Rita, in distancing herself from Mangold, uses a phrase which is similar to her first question adressed to Manfred: "Ist das schwer, so zu werden, wie Sie sind?" (12) Manfred, in his answer to her cry for help, resorts to Party jargon which is out of character: "'Jeder Fortschritt hat seinen Preis', sagte Manfred. 'Daß wir mit diesen Mangolds auskommen müssen, das ist unser Preis.'" (97) Rita finds more help in the Schwarzenbach family to whom she has turned first. It is Schwarzenbach's wife, a truly emancipated woman and mother of two children, who shares both work and family duties with her husband, and who protests most vigorously against Mangold's practices:

> Nein, dachte Rita. Ich glaub das nicht. Schwarzenbach sagt, man hat kein Recht, sie zu dulden. Er meint es ganz ernst, glaube ich. Und seine Frau erst! Die ist ganz wütend geworden. Sie oder wir! hat sie gesagt. Mit "wir" hat sie auch mich gemeint ...
> "Schwarzenbach ist Kommunist", sagte Manfred. "Aber du bist keiner. Soll er kämpfen, soviel und gegen wen er will. Aber was verlangt er von dir?"

to which Rita replies:

> "Ich weiß nicht. Er schien vorauszusetzen, daß wir in allen diesen Dingen einer Meinung sind." (97)

This dialogue reveals clearly that Manfred and Rita have already grown apart: while Manfred remains politically detached, Rita has in fact become part of a movement which is broader than the term Communism suggests. Characters and attitudes like Mangold's are seen to have a damaging effect on young, idealistic people for whom Socialism holds the promise of a better, more humane society. There are several examples in the book, where narrow dogmatic characters exert a damaging influence over those who, on the strength of their belief in a future for Socialism, have the courage to speak up critically against malpractices of the system. Martin is one of them, Manfred, in his early years before he met Rita, another.

Of the older generation it is Schwarzenbach who demonstrates this attitude most impressively for Rita. He had been instrumental in persuading her to become a teacher. (19 - 21) Yet it is a sign of Rita's development that Schwarzenbach turns to her when he faces a crisis after a clash with the authorities. In their final encounter (just before Rita has completed her recovery and is ready to leave the convalescent home), he asks her for advice and reassurance: was he right to attack the dogmatic Party attitudes in an article and incur Mangold's rage?

> "Wissen Sie, warum ich heute zu Ihnen gekommen bin?" fragte er. "Ich wollte wissen: Hat es Sinn, die Wahrheit, die man kennt, immer und unter allen Umständen zu sagen?"
> "Das wollten Sie von mir hören?"
> "Ja", sagt Schwarzenbach. "Ich habe es von Ihnen gehört."
> "Was ist denn los?" sagt Rita. "Warum haben Sie daran gezweifelt?"
> Schwarzenbach ist sich nicht zu schade für eine ehrliche Antwort. "Ich war unsicher geworden" ... Er habe einen Aufsatz in der pädagogischen Zeitschrift geschrieben, über Dogmatismus im Unterricht. Er schilderte falsche Methoden von Lehrern, auch an ihrem Institut. Er schrieb: Immer noch versuchen manche, zu diktieren, anstatt zu überzeugen. Aber wir brauchen keine Nachplapperer, sondern Sozialisten.
> "Ja", fragte Rita. "Was gibt es da zu zweifeln?" (185)

In her answer to Schwarzenbach, Rita is secure in the knowledge that both are striving for the same goal. She is less certain when dealing with Manfred's belated confession that he, too, had once clashed with the authorities. As a student, he had criticised the volume of unnecessary material and the dull, uninspired teaching methods at the university. In the showdown with the Party, in front of fellow students and staff, he was severely criticised; but worse, his best friend. a journalist, betrayed him in a newspaper article: "Er schrieb über die 'vom Leben abgekapselten, in bürgerlichen Irrmeinungen befangenen Intellektuellen, die unsere Universitäten in den ideologischen Sumpf zurückzerren wollen.'" (132)

Although developments have proved Manfred's criticism valid, he remains embittered, determined to apportion the blame for his disillusionment to those earlier dogmatic attitudes: "Er, er ist es gewesen, der mich zwang, dem Bild ähnlicher zu werden, das er da wider besseres Wissen von mir entworfen hat." (132) In contrast to the later scene with Schwarzenbach, Rita is unable to contradict Manfred, partly because she has not shared the disappointments of his generation, partly because she can find no arguments to counter his attitude, as we have demonstrated above. "Ich müßte ihm widersprechen, dachte sie. Aber was soll ich sagen? Ich nütze ihm nichts. Jetzt müßte ich älter sein, dachte sie unglücklich." (132)

Rita, too, experiences the full force of dogmatism and lack of solidarity among students when she supports her fellow student Sigrid who is punished by the Party for her parents' defection to the West. (Chapter 21) It is Schwarzenbach who comes to Rita's defence against Mangold in the ensuing tribunal. But she had already found the strength within herself to give up her attempt to escape to her home village and return to face the consequences. As she is being reprimanded publicly in front of her fellow students who, although ashamed, dare not speak up, she has enough detachment to recognize Mangold's performance as a sham:

> Mangold sprach lange. Rita wußte, was er sagen würde. Sie hörte kaum zu, aber sie sah ihn aufmerksam an. Er kam ihr wie entzaubert vor. Merkte denn niemand sonst, wie hohl jedes Wort aus seinem Munde klang? Wie lächerlich sein Pathos war? Ihr war, als könne sie den Mechanismus sehen, der diesen Menschen bewegte. (129)

Criticism of Party dogmatism was not common in the literature of the early 1960s, and Christa Wolf took a great step forward in separating the bad from the good, demonstrating how the wrong individual could do irreparable harm to the cause. Her candid portrayal of the black sheep in the Party, in particular Mangold, caused severe difficulties when it came to publication. But criticism was overthrown by the argument that Rita, after all, gains through her experiences and becomes more convinced in her attitude. This is demonstrated most forcefully in her final dialogue with Schwarzenbach where Rita appears as the character who holds the torch for truth and hope. She has gained this strength, the book suggests, through endurance of her own deep conflicts. But one must also take into account that the political situation in the GDR had changed with the closing of the Wall. It is against this background that this last dialogue takes place. Christa Wolf's point is that with the closing of the border, the GDR had to face up to its own internal conflicts. Dogmatism and rigid Party authoritarianism had to be confronted by those who still retained the hope that Socialism was there to work for the benefit of humanity, not against it. This is recognized as a power struggle, but one in which those who speak the truth can win:

> Die Leute, die ihn verdächtigen, haben mehr Macht als er, denkt Rita.
> Und Schwarzenbach, als habe er ihre Gedanken erraten, sagt: "Sollen sie ruhig noch ein paar Versammlungen machen und über mich schimpfen. Ich werde daran denken, wie gierig Sie nach Aufrichtigkeit sind. Ich werde sagen: Jawohl, wir haben eine besondere Lage. Zum ersten Mal sind wir reif, der Wahrheit ins Gesicht zu sehen. Das Schwere nicht in leicht umzudeuten, das Dunkle nicht in hell. Vertrauen nicht mißbrauchen ... Taktik - gewiß. Aber doch nur Taktik, die zur Wahrheit hinführt." (185)

Schwarzenbach's words reflect Christa Wolf's attitude in writing her own book. In exposing the harsh, sad, tragic situations in which the central characters find themselves, as part of an underlying move towards a better, stronger and more self-confident society made up of individuals like Rita, Wendland, Meternagel and Schwarzenbach, Wolf pursues what she, at that stage, recognizes as truth. It was this same underlying optimism and belief in the possibility to create a humane Socialism with truth and freedom as its roots which motivated Wolf and other like-minded authors in public speeches and proclamations in October and November of 1989, to call on their fellow citizens to ignore the opening in the Wall and to remain in the GDR in order to work towards this goal, as we shall discuss below. This would have also been the final test for an attitude like Rita's. Bearing this in mind, it is perhaps easier to understand why Christa Wolf remained in the GDR in the twenty eight years following the building of the Wall, despite the difficulties and obstacles a rigid and dogmatic Party put in her path. The character of Rita shows more poignantly than any other literary figure of Wolf's work how complex and traumatic it was to remain a committed Socialist and that it involved far more than a clear-cut decision for or against the GDR.

b) Meternagel and the Brigade Ermisch

The central position of the character of Meternagel in the book, and the crucial role he plays in Rita's development is emphasised by the fact that Rita's first outing after her return from the convalescent home is to him. The fact that he is reduced from an active, resilient man who brings about vital changes in the factory, to a weak invalid who has relinquished the opportunity to be put in charge again, makes it difficult to understand the central role he occupies through his initiative and forward-looking actions as a whole. Once again, Wolf goes against the established rules of Socialist Realism and the conventions of the "Betriebsroman" - the novel genre favoured in the 1950s - to demonstrate the leading role of the working class. Meternagel has moral and material victory on his side in the end. But the difficulties and obstacles put in his way are almost insurmountable, and to achieve his goal, Meternagel sacrifices all : family, material comfort, health.

Meternagel is in his late forties, but he appears much older, with more than one life history behind him. When Rita first meets him and he takes her under his wing, making it possible for her to adjust to work in the factory, he does not talk about himself, nor does he ask any questions about Rita's private life. It is through Manfred that Rita first learns the vital facts of Meternagel's past, his misfortunes and demotions, all tied up with the mistakes and errors of the first fifteen years of the GDR. For Manfred, Meternagel does not count as an individual, but rather as another indictment of his father's casual treatment and betrayal of people (41).

It is not until the final chapter that Rita learns from Meternagel's wife how much Meternagel has sacrificed to atone for his errors. (197) Details about Meternagel's childhood as one of five children brought up by his mother in a poor working class area where he had also met his wife who worked as a maid, indicate that he has never been allowed to shake off his milieu of poverty and excessive thrift. Seeing the aging women in her out-of-date clothes, bemoaning the sacrifices she has had to make of going without material comforts and household gadgets, Rita reflects : "Auch die Frau wird er hinter sich hergezogen haben, er hat nie etwas darüber gesagt. Wie lange reichen die Kräfte eines Menschen?" When she tries to convince Meternagel's wife of the crucial role her husband plays in the lives of others, she finds her loyal but resigned:

> "Sie können sich nicht vorstellen, was Ihr Mann leistet", sagt Rita, unfähig, die richtigen Worte zu finden, um die Frau zu trösten. "Wie sie ihn alle schätzen. Ohne ihn kommt man überhaupt nicht aus."
> "Ich weiß schon", sagt sie still. "Er muß so sein, wie er ist." (198)

Rita's last impression of Meternagel is of someone who has reached the limit of his strength and can no longer be part of the struggle that lies ahead: "Sie scheut sich, in sein erschöpftes Gesicht zu sehen. Sie zieht die Tür hinter sich zu." (198)

This seems indeed a negative comment to finish off Rita's story. Moreover, it does not convince the reader that she is looking ahead to a new life, albeit it in a more sober state of mind, as the epilogue suggests. Christa Wolf was heavily criticised for her portrayal of the character of Meternagel, especially by the brigade on whom she modelled Rita's work experience in the book. However, the pessimistic tone of the last scene is not characteristic of the role this character is given in the book. Rita's argument, "Ohne ihn kommt man überhaupt nicht aus", sums up her assessment of Meternagel's importance, not only in her own personal struggle, but above all as an example of someone who fights against the odds and succeeds. To understand this role and the significance of the character, one has to take account of what Meternagel himself sums up in the phrase: "Ich habe nämlich eine rückläufige Kaderentwicklung." (57)

When Rita challenges him to reveal his plan which he has drawn up in secret and based on his observations of mistakes made in the running of the factory, a bond of trust is established, and he gives her a critical and self-critical account of his political career, as someone who was pushed into a role as leader without being prepared for it (57-59). In many ways, his is a typical story of the working-class characters of early GDR stories who obtained a chance to gain a leading position after returning from a period of re-education as prisoners-of-war in Russia. Born in 1913 (in 1961, he is forty-eight years old [139]), he was of the right age to be called up at the beginning of World War II, and he spent the war years fighting at the front, having no say in the matter. After 1945, having served his time as prisoner-of-war in the Soviet Union where he was given a chance to pursue his own trade as a joiner again, he joined the newly formed SED as soon as he returned home. Unprepared for the leading office which was thrust upon him merely on the strength of his working-class background, he felt constantly out of his depth as he held a position of increasing power and responsibility. He lacked the experience of older Party members who had returned from exile, nor did he have the benefit of the knowledge acquired by younger people through rigorous Party training. Under this strain, he became a stranger to his wife and daughters and, ultimately, felt alienated from himself, being once again manipulated by forces beyond his grasp :

> Nur manchmal, in Augenblicken völliger Stille, fragte er sich wohl: Regiere ich das alles oder werde ich regiert? Er stieg und stieg und sah sich selbst dabei zu - bin ich das noch ? (58)

A serious error made him an easy target for the younger generation of Party members (the Mangolds?) who wanted rid of the older guard and demoted him, giving him back his old trade as leader of the joiners' brigade at the Waggonbauwerk. At the time Meternagel had recognized this step as both a personal injustice to himself and as necessary to the greater justice of the common good: "In seinem Sturz lag ebensoviel Gerechtigkeit gegenüber der Allgemeinheit wie Ungerechtigkeit ihm gegenüber, der der Allgemeinheit gedient hatte - selbstlos, das stand fest." (58) With Meternagel's self-effacing judgement (strongly reminiscent of Brecht's didactic play of his Communist period, *Die Maßnahme*), Wolf stresses the prevailing political and social Party concept of the 1950s: "Vom Ich zum Wir", subordinating the individual to the common cause of society. In Meternagel's case, society, i.e. the factory, has gained complete precedence over his private life, and as leader of the brigade he assumes responsibility, like a father over his family. When his own brigade betrays him over a sum of money which cannot be accounted for (a taboo which is kept veiled in secrecy for most of the book), his subsequent demotion to an ordinary member of the brigade under a new leader, Ermisch, is therefore a much harder blow to take, especially since Meternagel feels personally responsible and accountable for the money:

> Jetzt hatte er an einer Stelle versagt, die wie für ihn gemacht schien, jetzt gab es keine Entschuldigung. Geld war zuviel gezahlt worden, unter seiner Verantwortung, für Arbeitsgänge, die es seit Wochen nicht mehr gab. (58)

Meternagel is in fact the victim of an intrigue which was typical of the way in which those in charge disguised economic weaknesses to the outside by pretending that production was working to full capacity. The "famous" Brigade Ermisch which Rita joins when she begins work at the factory is in fact a sham, and the half-hidden irony with which the members refer to themselves is based on this knowledge. Ermisch is seen as the right person to fall in with the bogus game of receiving public honours, a mere puppet, as is apparent when the work undergoes a deep crisis. It is here that Meternagel, undefeated by personal and public punishment, comes into his own and sees his chance to vindicate himself.

Meternagel's fate in the factory is directly bound up with grave faults in the whole way in which industrial production was organized in the GDR. As part of the struggle in the 1950s to build up an industry again after heavy war losses and subsequent reparations paid to the Soviet Union (a further taboo subject in literature), and at the same time to be seen to compete successfully with the Federal Republic and its economic boom, figures were invented and production presented as artificially high. In reality, the drain of manpower and shortage of material and parts were a constant set-back. In the figure of Meternagel Christa Wolf shows someone who, undaunted by outside pressures on the larger political stage, has taken it upon himself to investigate and, with the help of a committed workforce, put things right in the factory. His secret plan, revealed at the right moment, is based on the willingness of the workers to increase productivity by building more windows in a shorter time. But what appears rational and logical to someone of Meternagel's sense of responsibility and work ethos is regarded by the others, in particular his rival Ermisch, as undermining the Party line. Far from being involved in the class struggle, the members of the brigade show no particular commitment to the work. Like most ordinary people they still look for a good wage packet and material benefits. This is, of course, a contradiction to the ideology of the new society of workers and peasants which, under Socialism, owns the means of production and is assumed to have a vested interest in steady progress.

The celebration of the 15th anniversary of the factory becoming "volkseigen" brings home this point. It takes the struggles and sacrifices of characters with outstanding qualities like Meternagel and Wendland to motivate the others. It is interesting to note here that, in her original plan for her book, outlined in *Dienstag, der 27. September*, Christa Wolf had one model for the two characters of Wendland and Meternagel in the master craftsman who has been sent to the factory for political rehabilitation (*Erzählungen* , 39. See also above). It is only when Wendland is put in charge of the factory, replacing the former work manager who has defected to the West, and when he becomes accountable for the sorry crisis and loss of production in the factory that Meternagel opens his book, revealing the wasted working hours over the period of a month. (73) He challenges the members of the brigade each to sign their name under a commitment to improve productivity. "'Verpflichtung' lasen alle. Anstatt acht Rahmen täglich, sollte jeder von ihnen zehn Rahmen pro Tag einbauen." (74) At first, the workers protest, not willing to break the official norm for which they had been rewarded in the past. But common resistance is gradually eroded as individual members, persuaded by Meternagel's non-threatening personal authority, sign the declaration one after the other until the brigade is united again in working with increased efficiency. The Party has no part in it, and even Wendland only lends support through approval. Rita, in reflecting back on the episode, discovers a photo which shows the brigade enjoying its new success, with Meternagel in the last row, behind all the others. (76) His aim is not to gain power and recognition for himself, but to bring out the best in others. In this, he shows a good deal of common sense and ability to deal with people in taking account of their individual character traits. His last, and most difficult adversary is Kuhl, a former Leutnant, who has not come to terms with his past and compensates by boasting about it. It is after Rita has accepted her own situation and is ready to return to her former life, that she relates this final triumph in Meternagel's fight. (193-6) The character of Kuhl and his role as the black sheep of the brigade is significant as a further indication of Christa Wolf's unwillingness to cover up the weaknesses in her society. This and other incidents show that the past cannot simply be erased but has to be addressed as part of the process of building up a new society.

As someone who learns from his own mistakes and is capable of making amends, Meternagel becomes Rita's most important guiding figure. As he introduces her to the workplace, so he teaches her to get involved in the ordinary, but burning issues of a society in upheaval. In this respect he has a more important and lasting effect on her than any of the other male characters. Her integration in the society of the GDR, presented in the novel as a process of growing up, is dependent on her understanding of Meternagel's struggle.

> Rita ahnte, daß sie erst jetzt die Schwelle zum wirklichen Erwachsensein überschritt, daß sie nun ein Reich betrat, in dem nur das Ergebnis über den Menschen entschied, nicht sein guter Wille, nicht einmal seine Anstrengung, wenn sie unzulänglich blieb.
> Gegen die Strenge eines solchen Lebens lehnte sie sich auf. (59 - 60)

In seeing Meternagel's determination to stand up to the rigours of this life while never losing his human touch, Rita is finally able to accept a similar severity for herself, keeping in mind the goal of a better, friendlier, more peaceful society. It is important that Meternagel teaches her not through words and rules, but by his example, and that this example also includes mistakes made in the course of his personal life. In trying to compensate for his neglect of his children, he is over-indulgent, and it is under his own roof that he allows one of his daughters, married to Wendland, to commit adultery. The ensuing rift between Wendland and Meternagel is healed through their joint efforts to lead the factory out of a crisis. Social commitment wins over family feud. This is shown when Meternagel and Wendland shake hands again at the party celebrating the factory's anniversary which coincides with the first completed production record in months. (86)

CHAPTER FIVE

a) *Der geteilte Himmel* and its critics

In 1965 a volume of some 300 pages of documentation was published by Mitteldeutscher Verlag (Halle) under the title *Der geteilte Himmel und seine Kritiker*.[1] It represents an important stage in the reception of Wolf's first major book since it documents the different reactions of literary critcs, the Party and ordinary readers in the GDR of the 1960s to a representative work by a contemporary writer. The editor Martin Reso, himself a literary critic in the GDR, selected thirty six reviews and articles which had appeared in GDR newspapers and periodicals, as well as on radio, between February 1963 and March 1964, with only two reviews by West German critics, and printed them in chronological order with an introduction and a postscript, but otherwise without comment. The articles range from approval to downright condemnation of the author and the work, and reflect the ideological climate at the time of its appearance. *Der geteilte Himmel* had already gone into its tenth edition and had been translated into five languages, one of them English (Seven Seas Edition), when Reso's volume went into print.

Reso quotes the first Minister of Culture, Johannes R. Becher, in referring to the GDR as a "Literaturgesellschaft", indicating that works of art have become a matter which concerns everybody in the new socialist society. (Reso, 7) Reso's documentation is a first of its kind in its focus on one work, and in covering new ground it attempts to give literary criticism a new status by drawing critics and readers into a dialogue. In the 1970s Reso's example was followed by editors of the main literary periodicals, *Sinn und Form*, *Weimarer Beiträge* and *Neue Deutsche Literatur* who used successive issues to print critical reviews and letters relating to new controversial works by contemporary authors, among them Plenzdorf's *Die neuen Leiden des jungen W.* and Wolf's *Kindheitsmuster*. It was Reso's idea that positive and negative responses should be discussed openly, whereas until then works by young writers on contemporary topics had been either largely ignored, or reviewed only if considered ideologically sound. Reso wanted to initiate a new form of literary criticism which combined socio-political with aesthetic criteria. In fact only very few among the reviews listed in the volume do address aesthetic aspects, one notable

[1] M. Reso (ed), *Der geteilte Himmel und seine Kritiker. Dokumentation mit einem Nachwort des Herausgebers*, (Halle [Saale], 1965).

example being Dieter Schlenstedt's article "Motive und Symbole in Christa Wolf's Erzählung 'Der geteilte Himmel'".[2] Reso places the debate in the context of a new phase in the cultural policies of the GDR, a response to the situation after the building of the Wall, which was regarded as the consolidation of the GDR as a separate national identity with its own "Nationalliteratur", differentiated from literature in the other Germany. Reso himself uses Party jargon in his introduction which makes one doubt his intention of opening a free debate among critics with widely diverging views without first giving guidance to the readers as to the spirit in which the debate was conceived. When Reso's book went into publication in 1965, *Der geteilte Himmel* had been accepted by the authorities and given its stamp of approval by being awarded the Heinrich-Mann-Preis. The defending speech by Professor Alfred Kurella of the East German Akademie der Künste was printed in full, and Hans Koch, a leading figure in the cultural policies of the day and member of the Central Committee of the SED, opened the volume. His article appeared under the suggestive title: "Sicher auf dem neuen Ufer", indicating that the GDR, secure in its identity since the building of the Wall, could now afford to have its conflicts openly discussed by young authors. (Reso, 11-15)

Two aspects of Wolf's book gave rise to controversy: her innovative style and narrative perspective and the political outlook of the author in handling conflicts in the story, in particular Rita's decision to stay in the GDR and Manfred's defection. The hardliners criticised Wolf's failure to give a convincing portrayal of the Communist characters in the book, notably Meternagel and Wendland. She was accused of a bourgeois, decadent outlook, reflected in the characters of Rita and Manfred, and of failure to put forward convincing arguments for Manfred to stay in the GDR. Her book was seen by some as too pessimistic and lacking in a Utopian perspective.

On the whole, however, there were many indications that critics welcomed what they considered a new beginning for literature, in particular Wolf's abilty to translate content into narrative form through the specific narrative perspective which gives insight into the individual's handling of social issues. In other words, some critics recognized the need to allow the author to bring her own experience to bear on sensitive political issues as long as the outcome was in favour of the new GDR society and against the decadent West. This seemed to be guaranteed by the author's comments in the prologue and epilogue and by Rita's process of finding herself in the socialist society.

[2] Reso, pp. 181 ff., first published in *Weimarer Beiträge* (Heft 1, 1964).

Der geteilte Himmel und seine Kritiker has dated more quickly than the work itself, but it remains an important documentation of the socio-political and cultural conditions under which Christa Wolf wrote her book.[3] Since then many critical accounts of *Der geteilte Himmel* have been written, in particular in West Germany where the book had a wide reception as a first serious attempt to offer insight into contemporary GDR society. The most comprehensive survey and critical assessment of how successive generations of literary critics rated Wolf's book is to be found in a recently published book on the reception of Wolf's work from the beginnings to the early 1970s. Katharina von Ankum, *Die Rezeption von Christa Wolf in Ost und West. Von 'Moskauer Novelle' bis 'Selbstversuch'*, Chapter 4: *Der geteilte Himmel*, puts the debate into a wider context of subsequent works, taking stock of literary criticism in both West-and East Germany from the vantage point of the post-GDR period.[4]

Ankum's critical survey, almost thirty years after *Der geteilte Himmel* was first published, of the important successive stages in the way Wolf's book was assessed in both East and West Germany is an indispensable guide to our understanding of the text. It begins with a full coverage of Reso's documentation, evaluating the different ideological positions behind conflicting critiques, pointing to the transitional nature of GDR literary criticism at that stage from narrow dogmatism to a more developed concept of critical Realism. In the mid-1960s the publication of Brecht's writings on literature in the GDR, in particular the Brecht-Lukács-Debate of the 1930s (published 1966), brought with it a more open attitude towards modern forms of writing, with an appreciation of Brecht's concept of realism and his montage technique. For the early West German reviewers Wolf's book marked the beginning of a serious interest in East German literature, firstly as a documentation of life in the other Germany, and secondly as a welcome sign of the author's disaffection with the State. A different, more appropriate approach came in the wake of the 1968 cultural and social revolution and its greater sympathy for Marxist positions.

Ankum gives a useful survey of major works of literary history and theory published in the GDR during the 1970s, which consolidate the notion of a "Nationalliteratur" on the basis of a revised concept of

---

[3] Reso also includes Konrad Wolf's comments on the film, in a local newspaper (*Märkische Volksstimme*, 24. Oct. 1963, Reso pp. 118 - 20).

[4] *Amsterdamer Publikationen zur Sprache und Literatur*, Band 98, (Amsterdam, 1992). For further useful comments on the history of criticism of all of Wolf's work, see also G. Kurpanik-Malinowska, *Christa Wolf. Zur Rezeptionsgeschichte ihrer Werke*, (Katowice, 1992).

Socialist Realism, and in which *Der geteilte Himmel* received extensive coverage. The book continued to be rated more highly than subsequent works, in particular the much more controversial *Nachdenken über Christa T.*, as Ankum remarks:

> Aus der Perspektive der Kulturpolitiker galt auch nach 1971 der *Geteilte Himmel* als repräsentativer für die Literatur der DDR als *Nachdenken über Christa T.* Dies veranschaulicht die eingangs aufgestellte These, daß sich Christa Wolf im *Geteilten Himmel* noch im Einklang mit dem offiziellen Literatur- und Sozialismusverständnis fand. (Ankum, 78)

Ankum points out that the 1980s brought not only a renewed interest in Wolf's book but also a different approach. Among the GDR critics she mentions in particular Therese Hörnigk's monograph of 1989 where the two novels of the 1960s are linked through the theme of self-realization as a process of individualisation rather than conformism. (Ankum, 79 - 80) Unlike Dieter Schlenstedt in 1965, who stresses that the conflicts are resolved, Hörnigk puts the emphasis on the need to bring the conflicts out into the open as a necessary step in the development of the individual. Where Hörnigk shows disapproval of Wolf's disregard of ecological problems in her portrayal of the industrial landscape, Ankum disagrees, pointing to the context of the increased emphasis on industrialisation of the early 1960s. Finally, Ankum is critical of what she detects as a tendency Hörnigk shares with critics in the West, to consider *Der geteilte Himmel* as part of a continuous development. (Ankum, 80)

In her extensive survey of West German critiques of Wolf's book Ankum includes important reviews and monographs which have established Wolf's position in the West as leading GDR author, (80 - 91) and she distinguishes these positively from the early reviews which find it difficult to reconcile Rita's motivation in staying in the GDR with the author's assumed criticism of the State: a problem area for both East and West German critics:

> Die Tatsache, daß Ritas Entscheidung für die DDR im wesentlichen Moment als gefühlsmäßig dargestellt wird, stößt im Osten wie im Westen auf Kritik. Dabei nehmen die Kritiker beider Seiten offensichtlich entgegengesetzte Standpunkte ein. Während die DDR-Kritik von Rita erwartet, daß sie, wenn sie schon Manfred nicht von der Republikflucht abbringen kann, doch zumindest eine intellektuelle Begründung für ihre eigene Entscheidung, in der DDR zu bleiben, liefert, bemängeln die westlichen Kritiker, daß Manfred keine Chance gegeben werde, die Vorteile des Westens Rita gegenüber darzulegen ... (Ankum, 85)

Ankum sees a direct parallel between the attitude of the early West German critics, and the responses to Wolf's text *Was bleibt*, published in 1990, which took the author to task for her ideological standpoint, while disregarding literary merits (Ankum, 86). Among the earliest critiques which viewed *Der geteilte Himmel* in the socio-historical context in which it was both set and written, Bernhard Greiner's *Die Literatur der Arbeitswelt* (Heidelberg, 1974) gets extensive coverage. Among the West German monographs which devote a whole chapter to *Der geteilte Himmel*, each with a different emphasis on the importance of the book for Wolf's development, Ankum mentions Alexander Stephan, *Christa Wolf*, (Munich, 1976) and Sonja Hilzinger, *Christa Wolf*, (Stuttgart, 1986). Ankum is critical of Hilzinger's interpretation of Rita as a character split between her emotional needs and the desire to adapt to her society. She regards this - basically feminist - approach as misrepresenting the author's position at the time of writing:

> Hilzinger unterstellt dabei, daß die Erfahrungen, die Rita in ihrem Industriepraktikum macht und die Gefühle, die sie mit den Menschen dort verbindet, weniger real und prägend seien als die Erlebnisse in ihrem Privatleben. Eine solche Opposition zwischen Privatem und Öffentlichem, zwischen Liebe und Arbeit scheint mir diesem Text der sozialistischen Literatur der frühen 60er Jahre nicht gerecht zu werden. (Ankum, 95)[5]

Ankum defines her own position as closest to those Western critics of the generation arising form the cultural revolt of 1968 who, on the basis of at least an openess towards Socialism, if not also a Marxist position, saw Wolf's book in the context of the social and cultural conditions under which it was written. But she is aware of the limitations which this approach imposes in effectively preventing the application of modern theories, i.e. structuralism, psychoanalysis and feminism.

> Daß es bis zu diesem Zeitpunkt weder psychoanalytische noch strukturalistische Untersuchungen zu Christa Wolfs Erzählung gibt, läßt vermuten, daß die westdeutschen Germanisten, ebenso wie ihre Kollegen in der DDR, den *Geteilten Himmel* im wesentlichen als kulturhistorisches Dokument der DDR-Literatur der frühen 60er Jahre einstufen und dessen literarischen Wert darüberhinaus relativ gering einschätzen. (Ankum, 95)

[5] Ankum is critical of Hilzinger's views which she regards as characteristic of the feminists among the critics who evaluate Wolf's work solely from the perspective of their own emancipation (pp. 94 - 95). It is surprising to find this dismissal of feminist positions in someone who was clearly influenced by American feminist views, as Ankum herself acknowledges in her reference to Sara Lennox in her foreword, and also in listing books and articles by American feminist critics Sara Lennox, Anna Kuhn, Myra Love in her extensive bibliography (p. 199).

Ankum's own way of opening up the deeper, more complex aspects of the narrative is through a comparison with the work that followed, *Nachdenken über Christa T.*. Consequently, she devotes the final section of her review to critical works which compare both books: ("Interpretationen im Vergleich mit *Nachdenken über Christa T.*", 96-101). The comparison leads to a greater awareness of Wolf's literary devices and influences absorbed in the process of writing. What is more, Ankum is right in pointing out that developments in Wolf's style in the 1960s make it necessary to reassess the concept of Socialist Realism. (Ankum, 100)

This leads to the question whether anything of note remains to be said about Wolf's book. Ankum identifies at least one area which has been neglected by critics who view the book in the cultural, social and political context. In her opinion not enough work has been done on the actual analysis of the text with a view to the question how form and content are related to each other. (Ankum, 95) It is in this respect that the present study can attempt to make a contribution to the on-going debate.

b) New Perspectives: Wolf's Story Today

Christa Wolf's *Der geteilte Himmel* is, as we have seen, closely bound up with the social and cultural history of the GDR. Successive generations of GDR critics have claimed the book as part of their national literary heritage. As Ankum concludes: "Selbst in der Rezeption der DDR-Germanistik der 80er Jahre gilt *Der geteilte Himmel* noch als repräsentives Werk der sozialistischen Nationalliteratur." (Ankum, 101)

Coinciding with the 40th Anniversary of the GDR, the film of the book, first shown in 1965, was again screened in October 1989 in Leipzig where riot police swarmed in the streets to control the people who were demonstrating for a more democratic GDR, for free travel and free elections. Their protest, it should be noted, was also an expression of their determination to stay: "Wir bleiben hier" became one of their slogans directed against the thousands who had left the GDR via the open border in Hungary and Austria since August 1989. In this situation Christa Wolf's story suddenly gained a new meaning for the people faced with a similar decision. The present author experienced how the cinema audience was visibly and audibly moved by Rita's desperate attempts to make Manfred see her truth: that the GDR offered the better future for both of them. As in 1963, the emotional appeal, not rational arguments, transmitted the message and made Rita's decision the more appealing one.

With the opening of the Wall on 9 November 1989, Unification in October 1990, followed by the first all-German elections since 1933, the 'other', socialist Germany has ceased to exist and with it the agonizing choice for those who, like Rita, felt a strong affinity with the country in which they grew up but who had to put up a hard fight to convince others of their decision. Although the least autobiographical of Wolf's books, the author had put a great deal of her own commitment into the figure of Rita, and a similar commitment reappears in Wolf's articles and speeches of the autumn of 1989, collected in the volume *Reden im Herbst* (1990). [6] In her speech given at the demonstration on 4 November 1989 on Alexanderplatz, then the centre of East Berlin, Wolf, using the language created by the people around her for slogans and banners, described the state in which they found themselves as a "wakening dream":

> Also träumen wir mit hellwacher Vernunft.
> Stell dir vor, es ist Sozialismus, und keiner geht weg! Sehen aber die Bilder der immer noch Weggehenden, fragen uns: Was tun? Und hören als Echo die Antwort: Was tun! ...
> Vorschlag für den Ersten Mai:
> Die Führung zieht am Volk vorbei.
> Unglaubliche Wandlungen. Das "Staatsvolk der DDR" geht auf die Straße, um sich als - Volk zu erkennen. Und dies ist für mich der wichtigste Satz dieser letzten Wochen - der tausendfache Ruf: "Wir - sind - das - Volk!" ('Sprache der Wende', *Reden im Herbst*, 120-121).

What is striking about the tone of this speech is that after forty years of mixed reception and much rejection and harassment, Wolf still identifies with the socialist society and remains as committed as Rita in her struggle to convince others. What comes through is the pure, almost naive idealism of Wolf's vision, her deep belief in human nature when left to make its own choices. In November 1989 Christa Wolf had many on her side who believed that the GDR could change into a democracy and who said so with a missionary zeal. In an article in the GDR newspaper *Wochenpost* of 21 October 1989 Wolf reports on a reading and discussion with teachers from a rural community in Mecklenburg

[6] Christa Wolf, *Reden im Herbst*, (Berlin and Weimar, 1990). Also as *Christa Wolf im Dialog. Aktuelle Texte*, (Frankfurt/Main, 1990). C. Wolf's article, "Das haben wir nicht gelernt" also appeared in a volume of letters addressed to her in the autumn of 1989: *Angepaßt oder mündig? Briefe an Christa Wolf im Herbst 1989*, (Berlin, 1990).

under the title "Das haben wir nicht gelernt." (*Reden im Herbst*, 93-7) She particularly mentions a woman of about sixty years, her own age, a teacher as Rita might have become, who deeply regrets the deformations which were brought about by the education system which taught young people to adapt and conform, suppressing their own spontaneous feelings.

> "Was haben wir falsch gemacht?" fragte in der Lehrerversammlung ... eine etwa sechzigjährige Frau. Sie sprach davon, wie stark ihr eigenes Leben mit der Entwicklung dieses Staates verwoben ist; wie sie an den Zielen hängt, für die sie sich in ihrer Jugend engagierte. Ich verstand sie gut. Natürlich will sie nicht vierzig Jahre ihres Lebens negieren; natürlich wollen und können wir nicht vierzig Jahre Geschichte löschen. Aber es steht uns eine schwere Arbeit bevor: die Vorausssetzungen dieser Geschichte und ihren Ablauf Etappe für Etappe, Dokument für Dokument im Lichte ihrer Ergebnisse und der Forderung des heutigen Tages neu zu untersuchen. Dabei wird eine Menge nur noch von wenigen geglaubter Dogmen fallen, unter anderem das Dogma von den "Siegern der Geschichte". (95)

The way forward, as Christa Wolf suggests here, is by confronting the past, not only the Nazi past, as she had attempted in *Kindheitsmuster*, but also the anti-fascist attitudes of those in leading positions who had proclaimed the victory of Socialism over Fascism, thereby preventing the ordinary people from taking responsibility for their own past:

> Eine kleine Gruppe von Antifaschisten, die das Land regierte, hat ihr Siegesbewußtsein zu irgendeinem nicht genau zu bestimmenden Zeitpunkt aus pragmatischen Gründen auf die ganze Bevölkerung übertragen. Die "Sieger der Geschichte" hörten auf, sich mit ihrer wirklichen Vergangenheit, der der Mitläufer, der Verführten, der Gläubigen in der Zeit des Nationalsozialismus auseinanderzusetzen. Ihren Kindern erzählten sie meistens wenig oder nichts von ihrer eigenen Kindheit und Jugend. Ihr untergründig schlechtes Gewissen machte sie ungeeignet, sich den stalinistischen Strukturen und Denkweisen zu widersetzen, die lange Zeit als Prüfstein für "Parteilichkeit" und "Linientreue" galten und bis heute nicht radikal und öffentlich aufgegeben wurden. Die Kinder dieser Eltern, nun schon ganz und gar "Kinder der DDR", selbstunsicher, entmündigt, häufig in ihrer Würde verletzt, wenig geübt, sich in Konflikten zu behaupten, gegen unerträgliche Zumutungen Widerstand zu leisten, konnten wiederum ihren Kindern nicht genug Rückhalt geben, ihnen nicht das Kreuz stärken, ihnen, außer dem Drang nach guten Zensuren, keine Werte vermitteln, an denen sie sich hätten orientieren können. ('Das haben wir nicht gelernt', *Reden* , 96)

Wolf's description of the predicament in which the first generation of "Kinder der DDR" found themselves is strongly reminiscent of Manfred. The parents and teachers, those who claimed to be "Sieger der Geschichte" and to have history on their side, were the adults from whom Christa Wolf and her contemporaries received their induction into Socialism. Their bad conscience, because of their own part in the past, had prevented them from standing up to the pressures of Stalinism in their own country. The analysis of the role of her superiors during her own formative years suggests that Wolf herself may have experienced a split in her personality: there is, on the one hand, her idealism and faith in the new society and humanity, based on Marxist Utopian principles, on the other her deformation by those to whom she looked up as leaders and teachers. As we have shown, in *Der geteilte Himmel* this split is related to two different characters, Rita and Manfred. The generation gap between them to which Manfred frequently refers - "Alle 10 Jahre beginnt wohl eine neue Generation" - seems less significant in view of Wolf's criticism of the parent-and-teacher generation responsible for their predicament. Manfred's story, but also Rita's childhood and youth, can be read with hindsight as a clear reflection of the parent generation's unresolved relationship to the past of deceit and self-deceit. Moreover, as Christa Wolf says, this process continued through successive generations and encouraged the young to develop split personalities. *Der geteilte Himmel* is a text which was written at the hight of Stalinist attitudes in the GDR. To what extent cultural policies were influenced by these attitudes became apparent in the mid-1960s with the 11th Plenum and the subsequent persecution of writers and artists who did not conform to the required partisan standards. Many documents have come to light since "Die Wende", among them much material which changes our picture of Christa Wolf in those years. As we mentioned in the opening chapter to the present volume, her letters to Brigitte Reimann, *Sei gegrüßt und lebe*, her speech at the 11th Plenum (published in *Kahlschlag*) and her own memories of that event (in the same volume) are documents which clearly indicate how aware she had become of the deep conflicts for those who had committed themselves to Socialism. With hindsight, the conflicts are there for us to see in Rita's story. The heated debate documented in *Der geteilte Himmel und seine Kritiker* testifies that the authorities were not deceived by the positive ending of the book. Christa Wolf has of late been accused of having an exaggerated need for harmony. Rita's agonizing reflections indicate at what price harmony is achieved. She is not a "typical" positive figure, but a complex and self-critical character with too much depth for her own good.

What, then, are we to make of Christa Wolf's recent admission that she had been an unofficial informer to the Stasi between 1959 and 1962, the years when *Der geteilte Himmel* was conceived and written? Here we are at risk of speculation with little verifiable evidence, except what Christa Wolf has made public. Wolf herself has always been the most severe critic of her early works, *Moskauer Novelle* and *Der geteilte Himmel* which she considered in retrospect as immature and untypical for her later writing.[7] The striking difference in style and narrative approach between *Der geteilte Himmel* on the one hand, and 'Juninachmittag' and *Nachdenken über Christa T.* on the other, is already an indication that the author had reached a more mature, independent form of self-expression, reflected also in her need to write in the first person. Here, we follow Manfred Durzak's view (reported by Ankum) that the weakness of the earlier book reflects the conflict between Christa Wolf's literary background and her Marxist views: "Das gleichsam neoromantische, verinnerlichte Literatur- und Naturverständnis widerspreche der didaktischen Aussage der Erzählung. In *Nachdenken über Christa T.* werde der Widerspruch zwischen Stil und Anspruch des Texts durch erzähltechnische Handhabung hingegen überwunden." (Ankum, 99-100) Yet, as we have attempted to show in the detailed analysis of the characters, *Der geteilte Himmel* cannot just be dismmissed as an immature work, an error of judgement of the real situation and the product of misguided idealism. We are inclined to agree with Ankum's view: "Erst nach der Veröffentlichung von *Nachdenken über Christa T.*, dem Text, der Wolfs utopisches Sozialismusverständnis am deutlichsten vor Augen führt, wurde die frühere Erzählung als entscheidende Entwicklungsstufe zu einem neuen Konzept sozialistischer und dabei weniger stark DDR-gebundener Literatur für westliche Interpreten interessant." (Ankum, 101)

Rita, and Christa Wolf, paid the price for their faith in what they saw as the only possible future which made them turn a blind eye to the apparent malpractices in reaching this goal - Rita by losing the person whom she loved, Christa Wolf by compromising her integrity, if only for a short period. In the final analysis *Der geteilte Himmel* still contains the material for our understanding of this antagonizing process.

[7] C. Wolf, "Über Sinn und Unsinn von Naivität" in *Die Dimension des Autors*, Vol. 1, 42 ff.

Select Bibliography

Primary Sources

Wolf, Christa, *Der geteilte Himmel*. Erzählung, (Halle [Saale]: Mitteldeutscher Verlag, 1963).
Wolf, Christa, *Der geteilte Himmel*. Erzählung, (Leipzig: Reclam, 1964).
Wolf, Christa, *Der geteilte Himmel*. Roman, (Reinbek bei Hamburg: Rowohlt-Taschenbuch-Verlag, 1968).
Wolf, Christa, *Der geteilte Himmel*. Erzählung. (München: Deutscher Taschenbuch-Verlag, 1973 [dtv 915]); 3. Aufl. 1974, 15. Aufl. 1982.
(All quotations referring to *Der geteilte Himmel* are based on the latter edition.)
Cardinal, Agnes (ed.), *Der geteilte Himmel*, (London: Methuen Educational Ltd., 1987) in the series Methuen's Twentieth Century German Texts.
Divided Heaven. A Novel of Germany Today, transl. by Joan Becker, (Berlin: Seven Seas Publishers, 1965). Reprinted in 1968. Reprinted also in 1976 by Adler's Foreign Books, New York.
Wolf, Christa, *Nachdenken über Christa T.*, (Halle [Saale]: Mitteldeutscher Verlag, 1968); 2. Aufl. 1972. West German edition: Neuwied: Berlin (West): Luchterhand, 1969.
The Quest for Christa T., transl. by Christopher Middleton, (London: 1971). Reprinted by Virago, 1982.
Wolf, Christa, *Lesen und Schreiben. Aufsätze und Betrachtungen*, (Berlin and Weimar: Aufbau, 1972). West German edition: Darmstadt and Neuwied: Luchterhand, 1972.
The Reader and the Writer. Essays, Sketches, Memories, transl. by Joan Becker, (New York: Signet, 1977) (Berlin: Seven Seas Publishers, 1977).
Wolf, Christa, *Lesen und Schreiben. Neue Sammlung, Essays, Aufsätze, Reden*, (Darmstadt and Neuwied: Luchterhand, 1980).
Wolf, Christa, *Die Dimension des Autors. Essays und Aufsätze, Reden und Gespräche 1959-1985*, selected by Angela Drescher, (Berlin and Weimar: Aufbau, 1986) 2 Vols. (Quotations in this text are from this edition.)
Wolf, Christa, *Die Dimension des Autors. Essays und Aufsätze, Reden und Gespräche 1959-1985*, (Darmstadt and Neuwied: Luchterhand, 1987).
Wolf, Christa, *The Fourth Dimension : Interviews with Christa Wolf*, transl. by Hilary Pilkington, with an introduction by Karin McPherson, (London and New York: Verso, 1988).
Wolf, Christa, *The Author's Dimension: Selected Essays*, with an Introduction by Grace Paley, transl. by Jan van Heurck and edited by Alexander Stephan, (New York: Farrar, Straus and Giroux, 1993).
Wolf, Christa, *Kindheitsmuster*, (Berlin and Weimar: Aufbau, 1976, and Darmstadt and Neuwied: Luchterhand, 1977).
A Model Childhood, transl. by Ursula Molinaro and Hedwig Rappolt, (New York, 1980 and London: Virago, 1983). The title of later editions is *Patterns of Childhood*.
Wolf, Christa, *Gesammelte Erzählungen*, (Darmstadt and Neuwied: Luchterhand, 1980) which includes: 'Dienstag, der 27. September' (1960); 'Juninachmittag' (1965); 'Unter den Linden' (1969). Quotations in this text are taken from the 1980 edition.
Wolf, Christa, *Unter den Linden. Drei unwahrscheinliche Geschichten*, (Berlin and Weimar: Aufbau, 1974).

Wolf, Christa, *Kassandra. Vier Vorlesungen. Eine Erzählung*, (Berlin and Weimar: Aufbau, 1983 [censored edition] and Darmstadt and Neuwied: Luchterhand, 1983 [complete edition]).
Cassandra. A Novel and Four Essays, transl. by Jan van Heurck, (New York, 1984 and London: Virago, 1984).
Wolf, Christa, *Störfall. Nachrichten eines Tages*, (Berlin and Weimar: Aufbau-Verlag, 1987 and Darmstadt and Neuwied: Luchterhand, 1987).
Accident: A Day's News, transl. by H. Schwarzbauer and R Takvorian, (London: Virago, 1989).
Wolf, Christa, *Reden im Herbst*, (Berlin and Weimar: Aufbau, 1990) also as *Christa Wolf Im Dialog. Aktuelle Texte*, (Frankfurt: Luchterhand, 1990).

Filmscripts for DEFA

Der geteilte Himmel, 1964. Director: Konrad Wolf. Script: Christa and Gerhard Wolf, Konrad Wolf, Willi Brückner, Kurt Barthel.
Fräulein Schmetterling, 1966. Director: Kurt Barthel. Script: Christa and Gerhard Wolf (discontinued).
Till Eulenspiegel, 1973. Director: Rainer Simon. Script: Christa and Gerhard Wolf.

Secondary Literature

Hilzinger, Sonja, *Christa Wolf*, (Stuttgart: Metzler, 1986).
Hörnigk, Therese, *Christa Wolf*, (Göttingen: Steidl, 1989 and Berlin/DDR: Volk und Wissen, 1989).
Stephan, Alexander, *Christa Wolf*, (München: Beck: *Edition Text und Kritik*, 1976) = Autorenbücher 4. 3rd revised edition: 1987 = Autorenbücher 603.
Sauer, Klaus (ed.), *Christa Wolf. Materialienbuch*, (Darmstadt and Neuwied: Luchterhand, 1979). New revised edition: 1983.
Drescher, Angela (ed.), *Christa Wolf. Ein Arbeitsbuch. Studien - Dokumente - Bibliographie*, (Berlin and Weimar: Aufbau, 1989).
Ankum, Katharina von, *Die Rezeption von Christa Wolf in Ost und West. Von 'Moskauer Novelle' bis 'Selbstversuch'*, (Amsterdam - Atlanta: Rodopi, 1992).
Reso, Martin, *Der geteilte Himmel und seine Kritiker. Dokumentation mit einem Nachwort des Herausgebers*, (Halle [Saale]: Mitteldeutscher Verlag, 1965).
Byg, Barton, "Geschichte, Trauer und weibliche Identität im Film: *Hiroshima mon amour* und *Der geteilte Himmel*" in Brandes, Ute (ed.), *Zwischen gestern und morgen: Schriftstellerinnen der DDR aus amerikanischer Sicht*, (Berlin, Bern, Frankfurt am Main, New York, Paris, Vienna: Lang, 1992), pp. 95ff..